"HOME FREE"

"HOME FREE"

Growing up in a Small Town in
South Central Pennsylvania

ANTHONY W. STRUBEL

MICHAEL W. ROTHAN

iUniverse, Inc.
New York   Bloomington

iUniverse books may be ordered through booksellers or by contacting:

iUniverse
1663 Liberty Drive
Bloomington, IN 47403
www.iuniverse.com
1-800-Authors (1-800-288-4677)

ISBN: 978-1-4401-3900-0 (pbk)
ISBN: 978-1-4401-3901-7 (ebk)

Printed in the United States of America
iUniverse rev. date: 5/20/09

For my nephews and nieces:
Krystopher, Mason, Eliana Trinidad, Logan, Kyle,
Celia, Sophia, and those yet to be born. This is the next
generation of "Home Free."

~ Uncle Mike

To my Mom and Dad,
for always seeing the best in me
and giving me room to grow.
And to my family, especially Mis, Tyler,
Brooke, & Nala who put up with me.

~ Tony

There will come a time when you believe everything is finished. That will be the beginning.

—Louis L'Amour, *Lonely on the Mountain* (Bantam)

179

Forward

What ever happened to the small town life: where a kid could be a kid and parents didn't have to worry about what they were doing or where they were? It seems that it was such a simple time…a fun time. I ask this because as I get older the days seem to get shorter and there is not enough time in the day to get everything done. But as I sit and reminisce about the days we had growing up, they seemed to last forever. Truly, the world would slow up so we could make the most out of each adventure that came our way. And as you became a little older and knew everything, you would feel like nothing could stop you or hurt you. I can say that we really made the most of that time we had together and I would not change a thing about those days; except maybe a little less of the hurting that always seemed to follow (i.e. you will understand what I am talking about as you read about the caves, the sledding/snowboarding and the inventions that *someone* had to try).

As I look back I guess you can't make a cake with out breaking a few eggs…arms, or legs. The "we" that I keep talking about was me and one of the most fun loving, honest, and caring people I ever had the joy and honor to meet and become best friends and blood brothers with named Mike. Who am I you may ask? My name is Tony. We have known each other ever since kindergarten where Mike use to take my play-doh (yes Mike it was not me that took it but you). There were not many days that you would not have found us together. We had become so close and inseparable that some people thought that we *were* brothers. In a way, they were right. We did become blood brothers in our early years. Most mornings and throughout the day you would have found one of us running through the neighbor's yard to get to the other's house (Sorry Mrs. Davies for scaring you that time I really didn't mean to do it).

When Mike came to me and told me he had started to write this book of our times growing up, I thought he was a little crazy for wanting to do this. Why would anyone want to read a book about two kids and their adventures as they grew up? But as we started to sit down and talk about the different stories we had and how they truly had an impact on our lives then and now, I could see how some one might just want to stop and read about a simpler time growing up; and perhaps even get a laugh out of the harmless trouble that we got ourselves into. I am also just as sure that we were not the only ones who had adventures with best friends; those people you spent most of your time with. I would like to take this moment to apologize to my mom and dad as well as to my other parents of that time, Mike's mom and dad. I hope you will find these stories funny and in good nature. I also hope that they answer some questions you have had for some years. I would like to also say that the schemes were all Mike's ideas. I was just the fall guy… literally. In all seriousness I want to thank you for always being there and helping us to become the men we are today.

I hope and pray that this book will help to remind you of a different time of life. A time that was much simpler compared to now. The worst thing we use to have to worry about was making it home before the sun would set and the street lights came on, so our parents wouldn't ground use for not making it home in time which would set us back for the next adventure. But none the less we would continue to have one adventure after another; Meanwhile learning all of life's lessons, and probably making a few of them up as we went along. I hope that these memories you are about to read bring you the sense of joy that it brought to Mike and myself.

Thank you:
Tony

Acknowledgment

Certainly, the two of us wish to thank
those neighbors and friends Tony and I
grew up with; our extended family, without
whom this story would not have been possible.

Thank you.

Table of Contents

Prologue

I was born, Michael William Rothan, on January 24, 1973. Tony was born two months before, November 22, 1972. He would constantly remind me of this when he thought I was being disrespectful to him (my elder). My parents were both originally from Kentucky, and moved up here shortly after they were married. My roots include, English, French, Irish, and German ancestors. My father's name is Richard Lynn Rothan, and my mother's name is Mary Anna Staples (maiden). I have an older brother (by one year) Joseph Lynn, who is married to Tammy Mitchell, and three younger sisters: Elaine Marie, who is married to David Romero; Elizabeth Ann who is married to Justin Quinn, and Theresa Marie who is married to Tom Adams. I have four nephews: Krystopher, Mason, Logan, and Kyle and three nieces: Eliana Trinidad, Celia, and Sophia with another niece or nephew on the way.

Tony's parents were Joyce Strickler (maiden) and George Strubel. He had an older sister Terry, who lives in Indiana now and Ted his brother. By the time I got to know Tony, Terry was out of the house and Ted was in high school, so I didn't interact too much with either of them. Tony's parents are my parents as well. And I know he would say the same about mine. It was on many occasions that Tony's dad would say: "Now Michael…com'on. What are you doing?" And then offer me some Amish root beer (which by the way should be noted, that it ferments and has similar properties to alcohol.) But I digress.

For kindergarten, I attended a public school, and my father, being the conservative Catholic that he was, insisted that I attend Sunday school for that year. From first grade until eighth grade (1979 - 1988) I attended St. Anthony of Padua Catholic Elementary School in Lancaster, PA. I continued at Lancaster Catholic High School on Juliet Avenue in Lancaster, for the next four years (1988 - 1991) during which time I studied mostly the sciences, drama, and was very involved in ministry. Tony was at Martin Meylin until High School. He went to Lampeter-Strasburg High School, or L-S for short. Most everyone in our small town went to that school.

Tony remained in the Lancaster area and took up sales. He was always gifted with people, as you will come to discover if you spend enough time in these pages. Upon graduation I entered Shippensburg University's pre-med program. I eventually transferred from pre - med to a straight Biology major, after deciding that I no longer wanted to be a veterinarian. I graduated in 1995 with a Bachelor's of Science in Biology. I decided that my great desire was to teach. I spent the next year and a half at Millersville University, after which I was certified in Biology and Chemistry.

Tony's first job was at the Strasburg pool. He was a lifeguard. This was a job that seemed to be made for him. Therefore, a lot of what we spoke about happened amidst happy bathers up at the pool. My first job was at Village Greens Miniature Golf Course in Strasburg, PA. It was shortly after this when I began to become interested in the bones. I was starting my own business with respect to the skeletal work. During college I worked for the dining hall, and in the Shippensburg University Vertebrate Museum as a technician, preparing skeletons and skins for mounting, and mounting specimens. I taught high school science for a year and a half and then I secured a position at a Catholic Elementary School where I taught for two years. I sold skeletons, and also worked for a cable show on some Sunday evenings until entering St. Vincent Seminary, August 19, 1999. All of these places and experiences play a part in the story.

I began to feel this calling again; a calling I had since third grade, toward the religious life. This calling slowly began to transition into a craving: a longing to serve God in an effort to become more like Christ; a longing that I could not ignore. I began to become much more serious in my faith, and to ask more questions, and pray more often. Prayer became my time with God, and I found miracles were occurring everyday. These were miracles that I had probably overlooked each day as simple coincidence.

Tony was married and had two children: Tyler and Brooke. Our relationship changed, not necessarily for the better or worse, but changed. I was away in college and working, he was at home and working, and yet there was always the connection. You know that connection with a friend…where you can get together and kinda pick up where you left off. The Greeks would call it koinonia, which really has no translation in English. It's kinda defined as "family" or "friend" or "twin" and yet each of those falls short. I know what it is, until you ask me to define it. That's why it's necessary to write a book about it. A word like koinonia is much like "Home Free." You gotta live it to know what I mean. And those who have lived it, really don't need an explanation.

Our childhood was probably the dream of most kids. Our greatest worry growing up in grade school was whether or not there would be enough daylight for my best friend and me to save the world, or build a hut, or go on whatever adventure day after day. Elementary childhood was a dream.

This forward is a thumbnail sketch, just so we can get started on the same page. And this book is only a antechamber to the world which is forever ours. There are many things that have been omitted for brevity; however, my complete autobiography will be out in a few years, and that will be unabridged. Our purpose was to tell the story so that others might benefit from it. And I must say: the three days Tony and I spent reading these pages out loud; laughing and crying…those were some of the best three days of my life.

If you will please read this book with an open mind, an open heart, and a touch of imagination. If you do, then you will come to discover something about me, that has made me who I am. None of us should ever have to journey alone. It's not how we're made…it's not how it's supposed to be. I can attest to the fact that in my life there have always been two sets of footprints in the sand. There are not many times when I can recall God not carrying me in one form or another. And there has never been a time when Tony has not walked alongside. For that... I am eternally indebted.

Michael W. Rothan
Written at Hermitage Pangaea, 17 February 2009.

CHAPTER ONE

An Introduction

This was it. Everything was set. I had modified a CO_2 pellet gun from Crosman. All I had was one shot. The grappling hook gun that I had created from this modified pellet gun was a crowning achievement. I mean really…how many kids had one of these? The grappling hook was not typical, in that it really had only one hook. I had taken a rod that had a barb at the end and laboriously curved it to make something that looked like a fishhook for "Jaws". Affixed to the hook (with a fishing knot ironically enough) was metal cable. This is the kind of cable that would normally be used to hang pictures, but the weight limit said one-hundred twenty pounds. How heavy was I now, one thirty-eight?

The pulley was pretty light weight, but sturdy. The plan was simple. Make a successful shot with the grappling gun, over one of the branches, and lock the hook. Then I would connect my end to the tree on whose branches I now stood and pulley across the creek. I was about twenty feet up, balancing on a branch of this sugar maple. The sun was blotched across my face like the spots on a fawn. The creek sounded so refreshing, I was tempted several times just to go back down, and "call it a day". *Maybe in the earlier days*; but things were different now. To back down from a challenge was not so simple, especially one I had been waiting for as long as I had. Days like this aren't incidental. I didn't wake up one day and just decide "This is the day". There were many days…many experiments leading up to this moment, and I was not going to be robbed because of fear.

I recalled the first time I saw this place…this sacred place. It was shown to me by another. He was a pilgrim to this place many times. I guess you couldn't call him a pilgrim since he was here so often. It might be called his home. Things were simpler then. A small town like ours didn't harbor the troubles one has when one grows up, or at least we didn't notice them then. Things were simpler.

The beads of sweat were coating my face like a film in this humid air. But there was air, yes, and it shook the leaves around me like so many cheering fans (or was that jeering fans)? They were all shouting the same thing: "Do it!" Two simple words with a world of consequence. I could taste the salt as the sweat broke free from my face. I was dressed in jeans and a shirt. I was wearing my hiking boots for ease of climbing the tree and now stood with one knee locked; my foot in the crotch of the branch and trunk, while the other was slightly forward balanced on the branch.

Man! Just thinking about all the crap I went through to get this gun apart and modify it to shoot a harpoon. It would use a whole cylinder, but it was worth it…if it worked. I had already tried the mechanism and fired the hook by itself days ago. It was relatively accurate and let out a pretty good pop; but, I had never tried it with the cable attached. I brought only one cylinder. It was going to be success or failure…no second try. This was it! Call it pride, I don't care, but it would work or it wouldn't. I froze as I heard something in the weeds. Was this an interloper? Someone who had followed me out here? I knew it wasn't

Tony, because he was working at the pool. I wasn't armed, save for a pocket knife… oh, and a harpoon with a zip line attached. I looked again, and then a cow moved around the bank. It reminded me of those people who get to the show early, so they can get a good seat. Well, this cow was in for a treat…she just didn't know it yet. Neither did I.

I was always one for inventing new things. I don't know what it was. I always thought of myself as this "brilliant idiot". The brilliance wasn't "book smarts" by any means, but more imagination. Amazing thing about imagination; it doesn't stay with you. Some people have imaginations that are so strong, they actually believe what they imagine. (This is without drugs, alcohol, etc.) What's more, they have such powerful imaginations that they can convince others of the same… even when they know otherwise. Mine was one of those minds. I used to see what was possible, and then try the impossible just to see. Tony didn't believe in the *impossible*. He told me: "There's no such thing as impossible. Just ain't been done yet, that's all". I suppose I began to believe that as well. The only limits we had in our lives at that time, were our imaginations. And at that time… they seemed limitless. I remembered I always wanted to fly…well, forget fly, I wanted to be Superman. I had made a costume when I was younger (of course I made it) and prayed one night: "Lord, if I sleep all night under this cape, then in the morning please give me the ability to fly." I really truly believed that would happen, with all my might. I woke up at some point in the middle of the night to go to the bathroom, and there was the cape on the floor. I had not made it through the whole night. I would never fly…unless, there was another way perhaps.

The cable was coiled around a cylinder that looked kind of like a spool. It took me long enough to coil it, and that was good. It meant that as the harpoon shot, the cable would spring from the cylinder and follow the path. The cable was an added weight, but the distance wasn't more than thirty feet, and like I said, it wasn't rope. The sun was high in the sky. It must have been about noon already…maybe later. Okay, enough of this. It was time to act. "On three. One"…the sweat dripped off my nose onto my sleeve. "Two"…I held the grip in my right hand and steadied with my left…I aimed high but the hook was oriented in the barrel down and the point was almost touching my left thumb. "Three"…with a POW! Like a small firecracker the gun spit the metal forward with nothing more than a puff of smoke. It was fast, faster than I had remembered. I heard the hollow sound of metal hitting wood and then a smile crept across my face. The hook had hit the tree off the left side and fell over a branch about fifteen feet off the ground. I was amazed at how the cable broke free from its coil and sailed through the air. The hook was dangling like a dead serpent over the branch of the tree. The easy part was complete…now for the work.

Slowly I began to retrieve the cable and hook, and as I did the cable wound through the bark of the tree. As I pulled, the hook spun as if the cable were unwinding itself. It would prove difficult to secure a single hook as it was spinning. This marionette, with only one string attached, danced, twirling again and again. I was only hoping it would tangle in the cable… that it would twirl around the cable, a *Cirque Du Soleil* hook, and then unwind again. The last time it wound I pulled as hard as I could. I took a chance and pulled tight and when I did, the hook caught under the wire and it was secure. I pulled on the cable to test the security, and although the hook seemed to give a little, the cable appeared to be anchored firmly around the branch. I pulled my end around the trunk of the tree and securely fastened it. The nice thing about cable, which is different from rope, is that it doesn't give. Once the cable is tight, it's about as loose as it's going to get. I assembled the pulley on the cable and was ready for part two.

The pulley was simple. Just a pulley, with a double handle below so that I could hold on with both hands. That was all. Now was the moment of truth. I had been successful up to this point. Now was challenge number two. I let go of the tree and gripped the pulley with both hands. My knuckles were white and the sweat was now irritating. It burned my eyes and was clouding my vision. I heard another movement in the grass: my friend the cow who was here to witness my success or failure. I shifted my footing on the branch so that I wouldn't trip, wouldn't get hung up, and was ready to spring. "One"… "two…" all I remember was the sound like a whip from a willow tree through the air… and then nothing.

CHAPTER TWO

The Caves

1

I froze. I couldn't believe what I had just witnessed. My best friend in the whole world; the only one who understood me; my blood brother; was lying lifeless on the pile of twisted metal below. He must have fallen about twenty feet if not more, and had landed on his back into a pile of metal and stones. I had no doubts that he was dead, or seriously injured. "Tony!" I yelled at the top of my lungs. Not a drawn out one like they do in the movies, but just his name, and then I waited. My body was numb. I lost all sense of what I was doing. I felt like screaming and crying, but knew that would do nothing to help Tony now.

2

In the memories of childhood, there always stands out a place where you spent a great deal of time, and a person with whom you spent that time. Whether it be an old house, or a field; a backyard or a sandbox, there was always that one place. It was a place at which your spirit soared, as did your imagination. It usually wasn't a place that another would find special or sacred necessarily, but always inspired you with feelings of adventure, and curiosity. I can remember only two such places in my life at which I was inspired, challenged, and perpetually in awe. The first of the two was this place Tony and I referred to as, "the caves." Although "the ruins" might have been a more appropriate title, "the caves" became a home away from home for us. It became a place where our spirits soared, and our imaginations reigned supreme. It became an extension of our dreams, and our aspirations. It was "our place".

Few places in our hometown could compare with this utopia for adventurers. "The caves" were actually part of a hillside that had been hollowed out for whatever reason, years before. We usually took a back road down to the area, which was less than a mile from my house. We would ride our bikes down the long hill, and then stow them in the drainage ditch along side the road, and camouflage them with weeds and branches. We would then carefully navigate through the briers and electrical fencing until we reached what was known only as the "home free" zone. After about a hundred yards through an open cow field littered with land mines (cow pies) we would behold the magnificent edifice. It was a hill that had been carved out, and the carved out part was sheer granite at some places, and grass and soil at others. There was miscellaneous junk scattered helter-skelter all over the hillside and along the cliff face. There were piles of useless tires, old hoses, fencing in rolls, old tractors and wagons, and slate was everywhere. It was as if someone designated this place as a landfill for the farmers, but without the fill. So much to see; so much to do, and so little time.

We observed, what we referred to as, three caves. One was to the left, at the base of the cliff face, and was about as wide as a five-gallon bucket. It started at ground level, and went further below the surface. This was the cave we spent the most time exploring. Many times we had reached the mouth of the "cave" but feared going much further because of…. well due to … um… well let's face it, we were scared. This cave got much more attention than the others due to the fact that it was exposed. The other two caves were covered with mounds of junk. We could see the entrance to one, but it was too coagulated with the remains of some machinery. Both of these last two caves were higher up on the edges of the hole in the side of the hill. When we stood on the top of the hill, it was about fifty feet to the ground, but not straight down. The grade was very steep and littered with all kinds of junk in most places, and so if we had fallen, we would have tumbled through much junk and twisted metal before meeting the ground up close and personal.

At this point in our lives, Tony and I identified with certain roles. He was the brawn, and I was the brain. This was not qualified in any visible way, although Tony was bigger than I back then, and probably was stronger, but we felt comfortable in these roles. We kept these roles, however, knowing all the while that each day I was teaching him, just as much as he was teaching me. We watched each others' backs like hawks, and were always ready for that unexpected dilemma. Such was the case on a nice fall day back in 1986.

Tony and I were still in the exploration stage down at the caves. We had done extensive studies on the smaller, ground level cave but none on the higher caves. Now I should probably clarify what *extensive studies* were. When you're young you learn a lot of that which you do, by observing others. We both watched quite a bit of TV and movies, as I said before, and in movies when scientists were studying something, they would measure, and make all types of instruments with which to take readings. We too did this. We used sticks, because the scientists on TV did, and I made gadgets with batteries, etc. that looked complicated, but really had no purpose at all. Most of the time, we ended up applying fuses to these contraptions, and then lighting them, with the hope that they might blow up in the cave and make the opening wider. To put it frankly, the cave was always in tact at the end of the day.

3

Having finished our extensive studies on the lower cave, we decided to tackle the other two. One obstacle remained in our paths, however. The two caves were up high on the cliff face, with little or no ledge on which to step. We would either have to scale the wall up to the cliff face, or descend from the top of the knoll. I had not yet made a device to help us stick to walls, so we decided the descent would be our best bet. The next question was how we were going to descend. As we were pondering this problem of physics, Tony spoke very softly. I didn't hear what he said, so I asked him to repeat it. He said: "I'll go down first. Once I'm sure it's safe, you can follow." I didn't follow. I mean... what he said. What did he mean? We didn't even figure out how we would get down the cliff face, and here he was volunteering. As all of this was wandering around in my head, I followed his gaze. His eyes were set on a target, as a hawk's on a vole. He was focused on a large oak tree at the top of the knoll.

The tree itself was on the rim of the cliff, just to the right of the little cave, and directly over the middle cave. If measured from the roots of the tree to the cave below, it would probably not exceed five feet. The roots protruded out from the carved-out hill, like the finger joints of a skeleton. Covering each of the "fingers" were tiny roots, like hairs, with soil clinging to them for dear life. This was your classic "haunted house" tree, with the setting to boot. It was approaching dusk, and if we didn't do something soon we would have to wait until the next day.

As I gazed at this oaken giant my eyes suddenly focused on another object. Around the massive trunk of the tree, there was a wire. This wire was the same type of wire used for the electrical fencing, but it appeared as if it were simply discarded, and found a dwelling place around this tree. As I continued my gaze, however, I soon realized that there was nothing haphazard about the location of this wire. Nothing at all.

The wire was around the trunk of the tree, and as I followed the wire toward the gnarled roots of the tree, I noticed that the free end of the wire was connected to a large rusted ring, and a long chain. The ring was out of proportion with both the chain and the wire. The chain had one and a half-inch links and the ring connecting the chain and the wire, was the diameter of a softball. The whole assembly shone a rusty brown color. I dropped my eyes from the tree, and looked at Tony. He quietly said again: "I'll go down first". And go down he did. We soon arrived at the top of the knoll, and looked out over our vast kingdom. Tony's face was emotionless, and I believe to this day that he did not look at me, because he was afraid I would try to talk him out of it… and he would have been right. The only time he finally looked at me was as I grabbed his hands, and lowered him down onto the rusty wire and chain. The last words I remember him saying were: "As soon as I get to the chain, I'll be home free".

I had heard this phrase before. I remember the first time I heard it I thought it was gloriously profound. It was glorious, because it was something that a "hero" would say. Much as Arnold would say: "I'll be back" or Hannible, "I love it when a plan comes together." The phrase was profound only in retrospect. Reflecting on our lives at a time when they were not bound by the worries and responsibilities of the world. I would hear this phrase many times, as will you in these pages. And yet as gloriously profound as it was, usually it signaled some kind of peril in our proximate future.

He was beginning his descent in mountain climbing style. As I said previously, we were both influenced very much by what we saw on TV. He held tight to the wire, and I saw the concentration on his face, mixed with a bit of uncertainty. I can't say what he was thinking at that moment, but his face told a story of its own. Tony would rarely if ever tell you that he was scared or anxious about anything; so I learned early on how to read his face. It helped sometimes to know what your partner was thinking, however, there were other times, that I wished I didn't know. As he began to crawl his feet up the cliff face, a waterfall of small stones and soil fell down the steep slope onto the junkyard below. His boots gripped the rock, and he began to lean back slightly so that the brunt of the weight would be pulling straight down on the wire lifeline. I heard the creaking of the wire as it lightly cut the rough bark of the oak tree, and saw rusty clouds jump from the wire thrown off by the pressure. Surely the wire wouldn't break under his weight. That was a strong wire, and the tree was solidly anchored into the ground above. Tony continued his descent.

Tony went down another foot. He was almost to the chain, and then it would be my turn. At this juncture I had accepted the fact that Tony was going to make it, and was now more anxious for myself than anything. What if I slipped, or the chain broke? What if we became stranded up on that ledge? I was focused on Tony as these thoughts ran through my head, and then I heard an unfamiliar sound. The creaking of the wire on the tree was the predominant sound and had been for the last few seconds; however, all of a sudden, I heard a snap. As I did, I saw Tony push himself away from the cliff face. His arms were waving through space, reaching for air as if it would support his weight. As he fell backwards away from the face, his legs continued to run through the air, while the heavy chain dropped into the abyss beneath him. I heard him yell for just a brief moment, and then the sound of his lifeless body crashing into metal, and soil below. Pebbles and loose junk tumbled down the cliff face in a cloudy landslide, and as the dust settled, all was silent.

I ran down the hillside and crawled over the junk to where this jumbled mass of limbs and clothing lay. I looked at his face, and his eyes were shut. He was breathing, but ceased to move. "Tony!" "Tony?" I couldn't believe it. I looked for blood, but saw nothing. I was worried about broken bones or internal bleeding, and was scanning his arms and legs. All of a sudden his head began to move. "Tony?" I said again, and he opened his eyes and looked at me. In that brief moment I saw into his mind. He didn't know where he was, or how he got here. He was waking up from a dream. "Owwww. My head hurts." were the first words out of his mouth. I was astounded. I was happy and overwhelmed with emotion at the same time. "What is your head made of anyway?" I asked half in jest, but all in earnest. He stood up and began to rub his head vigorously; as if he were giving himself and open handed *noogie*. He said everything else was okay, but he had a headache. This was just great to me. My friend would live to see another day.

We didn't get to explore the middle cave that day. Needless to say we were a bit disappointed. The wire had broken after all, and with it the one way to get to the middle cave. We decided that it was time to head home and check his head for any possible damage. Tony had flown without wings. Imagine. What I had tried to achieve by sleeping all night long with a Superman cape over me…he achieved in an instant. He rode the wind, and looked up at the clear blue sky. That moment appeared to last years, but happened in less than a few seconds. Tony had escaped fate once again, and it would not be the last time. He says that he remembered hearing the snap, and then blacked out. The first thing he saw when he opened his eyes, was me. He remarked at a later time, that what he had seen in my face, frightened him more than the fall. It was a look of dread… a look of loss. Maybe it is good that he doesn't remember much about that day. Some memories are best left in the far reaches of our minds. I, however, will never forget the day Tony, for just a moment, had wings.

4

The leaves on the trees were whispering their approval, as I had tightened my grip on the pulley and began my descent. Their whispering turned to a gasp as I heard the wire snap under my weight. The experience was unlike any other I have ever had. For a moment time stopped, and I was suspended in mid air. I heard nothing as my eyes looked up through the canopy like a green afghan with splotches of sunlight daring to penetrate the overstory. And then the afghan shot upwards with an urgency I didn't realize, until gravity slammed me to the ground. I was unable to breathe, unable to move. Was I alive or dead? Was this heaven? (I certainly hoped not, or maybe I was in the "other place".) I tried to scream, but only one word came to my lips. I had no breath with which to mutter, but my mouth feebly formed one word: "Heeeellllppp." And the one person I thought could help me; the one I had depended on for ages, was miles away, totally unaware.

CHAPTER THREE

Anthony "Tony" Strubel

1

Anthony William Strubel. Call him Tony, Tone, Antoine, Cochees, BA, Face, Batboy, Captain America, Maverick, Boss, Brother... he would answer to any of these with the utmost affection. There was a time, and still is on occasion, when all of these were a part of him. All of these made him the person he has come to be. I think Tony would agree (and I will ask him tonight) that these last thirty years have gone by in a flash of lightening, and continue to pass like a cloud on a windy day.

Tony and I met in kindergarten. As I write this story in 1997, our teacher Mrs. Mentzer, is still teaching. Wonderful teachers are like that. They can't quit, because they are so good no one will accept their resignation or retirement. "God bless you Mrs. Mentzer." My memories about kindergarten are a bit foggy, but I don't remember ever having had a negative experience there. I didn't interact much with Tony in those days, but he claims to this day that I used to steal his play-doh.

As far as I am concerned this is unsubstantiated. He has no evidence to support the claim. He would come to be the person closest to me, save for God. There is nothing he doesn't know about me. He has taught me every bit as much as I have taught him, and continues to teach me new things all the time. After kindergarten, I went to St. Anthony of Padua School in Lancaster County. Tony continued on at Lampeter–Strasburg School. Our reunion occurred probably about fifth grade. It was the summer of 1983.

My parents both worked back then, in order to put us through school and support us in all our endeavors. During the school year, this was not a problem, because we were taken care of during the day; however, during the summer it was a nightmare. If you cannot understand why, just check out the chapter on the caves, or the blowtorch. Our little town had decided, one summer, to create a recreation program, similar to the types of programs the inner city kids had. They wanted a program that would keep the kids until about noon, and engage them in various activities. The program was deemed the "SSRP" or *Strasburg Summer Recreation Program*. Most of the kids involved in this were from the local public school. I went to Catholic school in the city, and so knew very few of these individuals, but recognized some of them from kindergarten. I was not very athletically confident at that age, and spent my time more on inventing things, drawing, and discovery. I was more interested in forts, and making primitive traps, etc. like they did in the movies. For this reason, I didn't play a lot of the games that they organized for the other kids. So most of the time I hung out by myself. Every now and then, I would be joined by one or two others, but for the most part, I would watch over, or hang out with the younger kids, either helping out or otherwise occupying my time some how.

On one particular day, I was nosing around this baseball diamond. I had no reason to be there, because I was out of the sight of the counselors. Needless to say, I saw a figure walking around down behind the backdrop of the diamond. This was pretty far from the main counseling area, but I went back anyway and observed this kid. He had pale blond hair (it almost appeared white) and a dark body. He was pretty muscular for such a young kid, for he wasn't wearing anything but a pair of shorts some sneakers, and this old military hat. As I approached him, cautiously, he appeared to be in his own little world, and didn't notice me until I was very close. He looked up and focused on me with his crystalline blue eyes. He looked as though he were sizing me up, in case I were to "start trouble" or something. He said, "Hi". I said "hi" back, and then we just stood there looking at each other. Now I was sizing him up.

He looked familiar, but I couldn't place him for the life of me. Then he said it. "Weren't you in one of my classes?" "Nope; I don't think so." I told him that I went to Catholic school in the city. Then he said, "You look like someone I went to school with once". I told him I lived in Strasburg, and went to the pool and such. He went down this list of people asking me if I knew them or not, and I responded that I knew who they were just from baseball, and being in kinderga.... Then it hit.... "You were in my kindergarten class!" he said, and I actually saw a glow of light in his eyes, as if a circuit had just lit up. It now made sense. He was right. I remembered him now. His name was Tony--- Tony Scribble.

2

I had to get up. I had to assess the damage. My sight was blurry and I was sweating profusely. I looked to my left, and my left arm was bent at the elbow pointing up to the sky. But my arm was not standing on its own. It was leaning up against a fence post. It was one of those metal fence posts the farmers used for the electric fencing. I had missed it by only inches. I would have been one of Vlad the Impaler's decorations for Halloween if I had been a few more inches to the left. My right hand and arm were underneath my back, almost like a chicken-wing. Thank God, my hand had been back there to kind of cushion my back for the fall. I pulled my right arm around and almost passed out as a bright light shot through my sight. Pain and heat shot up my arm like so many hot coals. I held back a scream as I brought it around, so bad was the pain. Then, I looked at my arm. My hand and wrist were essentially relocated on top of my arm. I had a fracture of my wrist. I had to get back home. I had to get help, but the car I drove down here was a *Spectrum*...a stick shift. It was either that, or remain out here. I got myself to my feet, and began the journey back. My black and white mottled spectator looked for a moment as if to say: "Well... happy now?" and then continued munching on the lush grasses of the surrounding banks.

CHAPTER FOUR

A New Beginning with an Old Friend

1

"Well…you happy now? It's over." He had always questioned our relationship. I mean let's face it, he was always concerned about me. He could tell I was upset. Although I knew I woke him up, he altered his voice to sound as though he had been awake for hours. "What happened?" he asked. "It just didn't work. We tried, but it just didn't work." I was crying, and he knew it, try as I did, not to let it show in my voice. "Do you want me to come over there? Do you need me to be there, just say the word." "I know," I said. "No. I need time to think. Come over tomorrow night, and we'll have a palaver." "You sure?" he said, sounding helpless to do anything. "I'm sure man. Thanks." "Okay brother. You need anything, you call. I'll see you tomorrow night." "Goodbye," I said and hung up.

I don't remember too much about the call that night, only what he told me (so he must have been more aware than I gave him credit for). My girlfriend of three years (fiancée for one) and I broke up. It was over the phone; it was emotional, and I was truly devastated. I won't include the details in this story, because they are private, and belong to us. I still respect her and love her in a special way. As promised, the next night Tony came over and we began our walk, as was custom: each with a cigar, and a small ball about the size of a grapefruit. One would walk on one side of the street while the other crossed to the other side and we would walk and talk kicking the ball slowly between us as we went. The game was *Foosball*.

2

Watching my nephews and nieces, it never ceases to amaze me how they can take something so mundane, like a stick or a rock, and develop a game that will occupy them for the whole afternoon. And yet, I shouldn't be too surprised, because that's how Foosball got its start with us. We had been rafting down the little Pequea creek. At the end of the journey we found this rubber ball, about the size of a softball, floating in the midst of branches and snags. We picked it up as a souvenir of our journey that day only to rediscover it years later in my garage. One day, we were taking a walk, and Tony had brought the ball with him, for whatever reason. As we walked in the street along the squared-off curbs, we began to kick it across to each other. As we continued to walk, we actually began to develop point values for the kicks. If the ball hit the corner of the curb before hitting the street there was a point. If it hit and went out of bounds (in the grass) there was nothing. If you kicked it from the grass and made a good curb hit, it was double and then even sometimes triple. Every now and then, the ball would even hit the curb, bounce straight up, hit the curb again and then land, which brought the crowd to their feet (well…in our minds' eye anyway). That was the game. But the game was more about the walk and talk, than points.

3

These walks were few and far between because Tony was married with two children, which left little time for daily walks. His wife was always very supportive of our friendship, and I've come to love her as a part of him. We talked for the better part of two hours, well past the twilight, and at the end of our talk he said something that I would remember for the rest of my life. Something I never would've expected from him. All my life I had looked up to him. He was a good-looking guy, with a great personality, who attracted crowds wherever he went. He was smart, and athletically gifted, and I aspired to be those things he was. "Let me tell you something," he said with a seriousness I wasn't accustomed to, and yet one that demanded special attention. I had known him for about twenty years, and these moments I could count on one hand.

CHAPTER FIVE

Necessity is the Mother of Invention

1

I walked up along the path from the tree where I had plunged. That is when the laughter began. I don't know what it is, but when I'm in great pain, I laugh. Granted the laughter is usually amidst tears, but nonetheless I laugh. Sometimes people don't know how to take it. I know whenever I went to the doctor and something painful had to be done, they couldn't help but to smile, because I was laughing hysterically. I left the grappling gun and hook with the pulley, there. I really didn't even think of it until after the hard cast had been applied. I often think of going back there just for the flood of memories. We'd probably get shot these days. It's not like it once was. As I made that long journey back up to my car, holding my right hand and arm in my left, as though that would somehow make it feel better, I thought that it wasn't the first time an invention had gone awry. All for the sake of discovery.

2

Being the inventor that I was, I was constantly coming up with new things that Tony would end up trying out. I was good at inventing, and he was good at being a guinea pig… or tester. We were very much influenced by TV and movies back then, and would find a new niche almost daily. We were constantly in search of ways to make life exciting and adventurous therefore on many an occasion, we created our own adventures. Although this was not on the list to create, it became quite an adventure in and of itself.

The invention on that particular day was a blowtorch. It is obvious to kids, at a certain age, that some things we have access to are flammable. Some are even potentially explosive. Although at the time, I knew not how dangerous our activities were, Tony had complete trust in me, and what I knew about fire and its properties. I had trust in me as well even though I hadn't the foggiest idea what I was doing most of the time with this stuff. The invention was simple: an empty Spray 'n' Wash bottle filled with a flammable liquid. We would need an igniter in the form of a match and then someone brave enough to test it out. The liquid of choice turned out to be good old fuel, and the Spray 'n' Wash bottle did fine as an incendiary device. The fuel housed in the bottle could be squirted in a mist or stream and ignited easily enough if a match or other source of fire were placed near the stream. The time of testing had arrived, and we both braced ourselves for the unexpected.

Tony held the bottle at arms length away from his body and prepared to release a stream of fuel. I lit a match (taken from my house or his, I don't remember) and prepared for an inferno. I held the match loosely in front of the nozzle, ready to drop it as soon as I saw any sign of fire. I was daydreaming about my whole body catching fire, and just rolling and rolling trying to extinguish it, as I smelled that good smell of fuel on my clothes. I thought about how we would both have to live with burns all over our bodies and how others would look at us, and make fun of us, because of some stupid childhood venture.

I held the match in front of the nozzle and Tony began the count. When we reached "three", he would pull the trigger, and we would make history… for us anyhow. "One." His hand was as stiff as a board and his finger did not falter on the trigger. "Two." I began to move the match closer to the end of the nozzle, all the while thinking to myself, "Don't say it Tone. Don't say 'three' and we can go home as if nothing ever happened. We can forget about the burns, the agony. We can ditch the bottle with the rest of the trash and just continue innocently to explore… We can…"… "Three!"

"……Three." What happened? Nothing came out of the bottle. The lock was on. I blew out the match, which had been quickly approaching my finger, and settled on the fact that I probably wouldn't have to light another one today. I was mistaken. The nozzle's adjustment was screwed all of the way in, allowing no fuel to pass. Was this an omen? Would this be just enough for us to call it quits? No. Tony simply loosened the adjustment, and began to count again. "One." I lit a second match. It took me two strikes to get a light. As if once wasn't enough, I had to repeat this agonizingly exciting venture. "Two." This was it. No mistakes this time. No way out. It was all or none. "Three!" With that three came a little squeak and then a six foot tongue of flame leapt from the nozzle of the Spray 'n' Wash bottle into the air, as if it were a genie trapped for a thousand years. The fire was a bright yellow flame, with a roaring intensity. It made the sound of thunder as it lunged from the bottle toward freedom. As Tony's finger released the trigger, the beast dissolved just as quickly as it had leapt. The match had been extinguished, and all that remained in the air was the faint smell of fresh fuel and small tongues of smoke. We both looked at each other in a way that could only be described as blind wonderment. A similar sight was probably witnessed by animals a few million years ago, when prehistoric man first discovered fire.

We were beside ourselves. It worked! It actually worked! We had created something that, to this point, we had only seen in movies and on TV. We had invented something that was brilliant, but simple in the same respect. We had tested and had wonderful results… now what? We began to experiment with different things and how they burned. Cloth, leaves, plastic, and metal, were all among the things tested. Although this invention was attractive to us, we soon became aware of how awesome, and potentially destructive it could be. But this invention wasn't nearly the most dangerous weapon.

CHAPTER SIX

Held at Gunpoint

1

Growing up in an area where many Amish lived, it also wasn't the first time we had tested inventions on Amish property and something bad happened. Some things we do in life are stupid. Let's face it. Unfortunately, we don't realize *how* stupid these things actually are, until after they're done. Then we reap the consequences, lick our wounds, and snap back to our old selves again. Time does eventually heal most, if not all, wounds. Some things, however, we never quite forget.

Tony and I were down at the *caves* when such an event took place. I will never forget the day or the events leading up to this particular venture; although at the time, I tried very hard to forget. It was a calm autumn afternoon. The leaves had already changed and were just beginning to flutter aimlessly down from their lofty homes. Tony and I were of course in school, and were to meet after getting home, to talk about our next test of the blowtorch. Like most kids our age there was a certain fascination for fire. It was difficult for us to get fuel, so we would load up the bottle either before my parents got home, or before Tony's, but we usually could get the bottle about half full. (Now, a chemist, I realize how dangerous this actually was. In many fuels, FUMES can ignite just as well as liquid.) We mounted our trusty steeds, with Tony's wagon hooked up to one of our bikes, and began the trek down the long country hill to the caves.

When going to the caves, we never knew what kind of stuff we would run into, so we often brought the wagon in case we wanted to take some interesting *treasures* back with us. We rode down the long hill discussing what was in our future for this evening. We were going to spend some time down at the caves, and either he would eat at my house or *vice versa*. Either way, we usually shared a meal, not unlike most other things we had. We finally arrived at the caves, and we hid the bikes and wagon in the drainage ditch on the left side of the road as was common practice. We pushed the weeds down over the bikes and wagon, and then crossed the drainage ditch on the same side of the road to get to the caves. Around the perimeter of the caves was an electric fence. The caves served not only as a place of intrigue for us, but also as a cow field for a local Amish farmer. At this point, we began this venture as any other venture at the caves by quickly brushing the fence to see if the juice was on. Some days there were even cows walking on the other side, but not today. We touched the fence and discovered to our surprise that it was not on. This made life easier, however, Tony, in always trying to better himself, still made the attempt to get through the fence without making contact with the wire. "We are always in training", he used to say (still does at times). We navigated our way once again, through the fence and briers, and to the clearing with the manure land mines randomly scattered over the landscape. Then we began our approach, with Spray 'n' Wash bottle in hand. Tony had hooked the bottle to his belt by the trigger on the nozzle while he was crossing the fence line, and it now beat against his leg in a rhythmic pattern.

I had taken a book of matches that we had holed away. When we were kids, we were very observant. If one looked carefully, one could find matches, lighters, and other great junk in the most unlikely places. Matches were a very scarce commodity. We always had to conserve them. At one point, we even used birthday candles so that we could keep a flame lit, and would not use so many matches.

We arrived at the section that was the heart of the place where there was a small clearing surrounded by junk of every kind. Before we worked with the torch again, we certainly had to check out the mouth of the small cave for footprints or any other signs of life. As we looked into the small hole, neither of us was focused enough to notice whether anything was there or not. If there were the footprint of a yeti, we probably would have overlooked it completely. Our minds were centered on the mission at hand.

We began as always, with Tony being the guinea pig. I held the match and Tony squeezed the trigger, assured that this time the nozzle was not locked. A spout of flame shot out of the bottle, and it was as if we had never seen fire before. The match had been extinguished by the force of the flame, but the residual scent of spent fuel filled the air. The preliminary test was over. It was time to do some tests we had not yet done. We had decided that instead of holding the match and spraying, it might be interesting to put the match on the ground, and fire at it. Tony held the bottle about two feet from the ground. I lit the match and tossed it on the ground. The second the match hit the ground Tony squeezed the trigger, and… nothing happened. The match had gone out upon hitting the ground. There was a nice dark circle where the fuel had hit. The spent match was centered perfectly in the middle. We were ready to try again. I lit the match and decided that I would just throw it into the same spot on the ground. As the match left my hand, I think Tony suddenly came to a revelation. He yelled "wait", but it was too late. The match hit the spot of fuel and ignited into a ring of fire in an instant. In the next second, it was out. The fire had gone out just as quickly as it had ignited. We were in awe. We exchanged a look, and that was the beginning of the end.

When you've been friends with someone for as long as we have, words become irrelevant. You can communicate so much better with a look; a smile; or even a sign. Tony and I found most of the time, especially when sneaking out at night, that words many times just got in the way. When you're with a person for so long, and as friends you depend on each other for so much, it is almost as if your brains have their own frequency, and no one else uses that band.

Tony gave the bottle to me, and it was my turn to experiment. I pulled the trigger of the bottle three times quickly releasing a surge of fuel onto an old pile of slate. Tony tossed a match onto the sheen of fuel and the slate roared like a strong wind. It was now Tony's turn again. We were looking for something not yet attempted by our standards. As we were walking Tony stopped and looked. I followed his gaze, and although I didn't understand his idea completely, I knew that it would hold certain adventure for us. Little did I know how much adventure.

You can call it *Marmota monax,* groundhog, or woodchuck, but whatever you call it, we had a huge population of them in Strasburg. Now, although I mention my hometown of Strasburg, I believe these guys can be a pest anywhere; ask the character Bill Murray played in *Caddie Shack.* The caves were no exception to the rule. Groundhog holes riddled the landscape at the caves. I often wondered if any cow had broken a leg due to a groundhog hole. We decided, after having seen many groundhogs during our times at the caves, that we would try to drive one out of its hole. This was the idea Tony had come up with, and I was in for the ride.

We began as always, with a match, and the Spray 'n' Wash bottle. Tony held the bottle, and I the matches. Tony haphazardly sprayed the fuel around the groundhog hole until the ground was saturated with the stuff. I then lit a match, and lowered the match toward the ring of liquid. I was about eight or ten inches away when I released the match into the liquid ring. The match hit the ground and to our surprise the only sign that a match had even been lit was the faint gray threads of smoke rising from the dead match. I lit another match and dropped it onto the moist soil, however this time the moist soil erupted into a ring of fire around the hole. We were mesmerized by our small triumph, and began to brainstorm what we would do next. We continued across the concave face of the caves and onto a slightly more level base. We soaked the soil with our flammable fuel again, and ignited it in an orange ring of heat and charring fire. As this last ring began to flicker to a black ring on the ground, I felt a presence. A weird feeling came over me, and a chill passed down my spine. Was that feeling the cold stare of an interloper or an outsider? Were we being watched? We were.

2

When we consider how much stuff we got into, and how most of it was unknown to anyone but us, it is amazing. We were either very good at covering our tracks, or very lucky…or both. I remember my granddaddy made a go-cart for me and my brother. We brought it back from Kentucky, and our use of it was limited to driving up our driveway (which might have been about thirty feet) and coasting backwards until we made contact with the sidewalk again. My dad insisted that we where a helmet, so we had this bright yellow helmet. After a bit, Tony's Pap said we could ride up in his field. He was a

ANTHONY W. STRUBEL & MICHAEL W. ROTHAN

farmer and had a cornfield up near the pool. That was all we needed. We drove up there until we ran out of gas.

We were always careful…well, most of the time. But a few times, we were getting a little "dare-devilish" and thus careless. I remember two such cases where Tony, once again was the crash-test dummy; well at least a crash-test. He wanted to do a sprint on this go-cart to see how fast it could go. That thing could go pretty fast when it wanted to. Anyway, we were all taking turns, and as Tony came back, he went up on the embankment of the neighbor, and tore out a divot in his grass. He then took off down through the field. All I remember seeing is the go-cart fly forward, back over front and Tony like a rag doll fly off of the machine. I was up on the bank repairing the divot while the neighbor looked out the window watching. I began running to the overturned car thinking the worst possible scenario. As I was running, Tony sat up with his hands resting on his knees like a long-jumper who has fallen back into the sand. He was taking off the helmet as I approached and shaking his head as if he were trying to get water out of his ears.

"The wheels went like this," and his hands, with fingers straight up like he did when he was telling me how big the fish was that he caught, suddenly moved outward making a wide "V" sign. The steering rod between the wheels broke and the tires did their own thing, thus flipping him head over heals. He was fine, physically at least. He was fine, until we got back up to his Pap's house, and the neighbor was out, eyeing up the damage to his pristine lawn. The damage to Tony that day was minor. But it would not be the last time we were in the wrong place at the wrong time.

3

I slowly shifted my eyes upward, careful not to move my head, and saw him; a dark figure looming farther up the hillside in front of us. He could not have been but fifteen feet away, but the sun setting behind him created a black specter; a silhouette one might expect to see at the end of a western, or on an advertisement for cigarettes. The figure was only recognizable by the straight brim of his hat placed squarely on his head, and the very distinct form held tightly in his hands. The barrel was probably only about thirty inches long, but the shadow must have been thirty feet. The figure was motionless. If not for the perfect outline of his hat, he might as well have been a dead tree up on the hill. He remained motionless... the hunter, and as a deer caught in headlights, we too remained motionless... the prey.

I had a habit of being the center of attention at family gatherings, and parties, because... well um... well because I was the center of attention. I was a *ham*. If there were something to be done, a camera would be focused, and I would perform with little to no provocation. One of my performances was done with the aid of a ventriloquist doll by the name of Charlie McCarthey. I was fairly good at throwing my voice, or so I was told at the time. At this moment I really needed that ability to throw my voice and not let the figure above know it. Where was my talent for ventriloquism now? Why could I not speak? Every time I attempted to speak, nothing would come to my mouth. Then I heard it. Just seven little words that would set my mind at ease... for the most part. Without looking, Tony stood motionless, and said under his breath: "I know. Let me do the talking." That was all she wrote.

Tony began with the phrase he was most comfortable with. The phrase with which he had met hundreds of girls. The phrase with which his whole script; his whole persona was based on. Three little words that could make the young girls go nuts and the old folks smile. "How ya doin?" It wasn't a question so much as it was a statement. The man in the hat looked stunned. It seemed like he hadn't expected that at all, or at least that's what we read in his expression. He approached us, and as he did he brought with him his more elucidated features.

One of those features I almost wish had remained hidden. That feature was also his most prominent one. The feature was made up of a dark iron barrel, and the polished wooden stock placed snugly in the pit of his arm. His left hand tightly grasped the hilt, and this right finger was just tickling the trigger. Our eyes finally met. He had stone blue eyes that were fixed on the two young boys standing dead in front of him… but not dead yet anyway. He couldn't have been older than sixteen and had a patchy scruff growing in at places on his face. His face was a young face; innocent and untarnished by worldly things. There was something else in his face though, something that would be our saving grace. Tony saw it too. Dancing in those stone blue eyes, amidst all of the other emotions… was fear. And we would use that to our advantage.

"What you boys be doin' down heah?" was all he could say. He tried to keep a steady voice, but the shakiness in his words was quite evident. "We're just walking around." Tony replied. His voice was as solid as the iron barrel on our adversary's gun, and as smooth as the wood grain stock. I thought to myself surely there was no way this guy; this kid, no matter how frightened he was, would believe that we were just "walking around". I gave the kid some credit, at least, and he didn't disappoint me. He reached up and slightly lifted his straw summer hat with this trigger hand as he hooked the gun underneath the hilt with his arm. The barrel was now safely pointed at the ground. As he lifted his hat, he took the same sleeved arm and wiped his forehead. In our nervousness, I hadn't realized how hot it actually was. He replaced his hat on his head and tilted it back slightly which gave him a look of exhaustion. His look more or less said that he had been working all day, and this was the last thing he wanted to deal with right now.

He looked at Tony and I followed the figure's eyes down to the bottle. He asked, "What's in the bottle?" How far could we get with these short answer questions? It seemed for every short question there was an even shorter lie. When you have a barrel pointed in your direction, however, you have little choice but to think fast. Tony responded with an answer that I could never have seen coming in a million years. The second part anyway, was about as far-fetched as it gets. "I don't know," he said. "We found the bottle down here."

For just an instant, I saw the glimpse of hope. The boy looked as if he wanted to believe us. He was looking for a way out, and we were handing it to him on a silver platter. The look he gave was almost one of compromise. Almost as if he were saying: *Look. I don't want to be here, I've never used a gun, and you just leave and promise never to come back, and I won't follow this up with anything.* He had decided to let us go. He may not have realized it yet, but we saw it in his eyes. Tony saw the weariness and helplessness in the eyes of the gun holder, and took the opportunity while it was ripe. "Listen," he said. "We were just walking around down here and found this bottle lying on the ground." The amishman then replied, "This is private property". Tony responded with the classic defense of many a criminal. Although this phrase rarely works in the courts anymore, it did work for us. Tony said, "We didn't know it was private property. We'll leave" (as if the electric fence shouldn't have tipped us off to the fact that it was someone else's land).

I couldn't believe it! We were walking out of this situation scot-free. No bruises, no scrapes, nothing but a minor scare. We were carefully maneuvering the cow pies, and groundhog holes, as we approached the final stretch of field. The electric fence, as ominous as ever, stretched before us bidding us farewell. As we were preparing to clear the fence and ride home as never before, Tony whispered, "Through the fence, and we're home free". This is not the first time Tony had said that we'd be "home free," and it certainly would not be the last. It seemed every time he believed we "had made it" or had to just make it down the final stretch, this was a phrase he thought would put us over the top. And yet, time and time again, it was usually the moment that something would go terribly wrong. This moment was no exception. I felt the presence again, and a chill swept over me for the second time that day.

The sound that broke the silence was that of feet briskly moving through the tall grass. The shuffle grew louder, and neither of us dared to acknowledge the source. We ignored the pursuer, stayed our course and quickened the pace. I felt like Icobod Crane as the bridge he had to cross in order to stay his execution from the Headless Horseman, was in his sights. The pursuit stopped abruptly, and a strange voice yelled "Hey!" We froze. This was not the sheepish adolescent voice, that we had been previously introduced to. This was a new voice...a voice of authority.

4

"Hey!" I looked up from the car where I had arrived only moments before, holding my broken wrist and trying to stay on my legs. It was an amishman. "You aw right?" "Yeah," I shouted through clenched teeth, probably a little too well, attempting to bite back the tears and trying to hold in my laughter which had now reached delirious proportions. What would he do to help? Set the break with a fence post? Race me to the hospital with the horse and buggy? Don't get me wrong, I grew up with Amish and even had Amish friends. But let's be practical... the help I needed was a few miles away, and the only way to get there was to drive. I got into the car, which felt like a furnace, and opened my window. I thought I would be sick. I started the car and put it into gear, and began my journey along the blurry gray. Green and gray is all I saw, but the ride would be short, right? I reached over with my left hand as the engine lurched and shifted into second. It would be one of the longest rides of my life.

5

"Hey!" the amish boy shouted. Despite the way Tony and I were now double-timing it, he caught up with us, and sounded none-too-pleased. We both turned around as if we were synchronized swimmers in the gold medal event at the Olympics. Tony's hand gripped the bottle from which the trouble began. We weren't *home free* just yet. "Let me see that bottle." The voice had lost some of its authority, as we gazed on the sheepish boy we had dealt with previously. He must have had a burst of adrenaline for just a moment, and then realized how sheepish he actually was. Tony effortlessly tossed the bottle to the boy and began to think of what to do next. The fence was close enough, but he was still armed with that shot gun. Whether it housed shot, or just rock salt, we would easily get a hide-full of it, and we weren't in the mood to find out.

The boy unscrewed the lid, keeping his eyes on us the whole time. He lifted the bottle up to nose level and took a sniff. "Smells like gas-*ole*-leen." he stated in a lethargic sort of way. Now Tony was on the defensive. He saw a vision of the two of us sitting in jail for arson. "We found the bottle down here," he said. That part again wasn't too far fetched, but the next part was *out there*. "My mom collects Spray 'n' Wash bottles, and we were just bringing this one home to her." Well I just about dropped. I thought to myself, "This is the last time I ever let him talk us out of something". The Amish boy lazily screwed the top back on the bottle, gave one last look at us, and said, "Get on outa here now, and don't come back". What! That was it? No inquisition? He slowly turned and walked back toward where we had first met. All the while he was walking and looking at the bottle as if it were the first one he had ever seen. The gun was still clenched underneath his right arm. The sky was darkening, and the shadows were reaching for the ends of the earth. We didn't take a second look back. We darted through the fence and into the drainage ditch; we grabbed our bikes, and we pedaled as fast as our legs could carry us.

It was over. We had danced with danger and won. We never knew what happened with the boy afterwards: how his family reacted; whether they called the police; whether he even told them he found anyone at all. We just knew that we were scared straight. We no longer had the caves as a place we could test these incendiary devices. We had to find another. Sometimes we just need to be scared. I believe fear is what keeps good people *good* sometimes, and God-fearing people God-fearing. Out of all of this I learned an important lesson. Fear is relative. If used properly, it can be your greatest asset. If we succumb to it our downfall is sure.

CHAPTER SEVEN

First Encounters: Looking Back and the "B-team"

1

I'm glad Tony and I had been able to get together for this walk. I listened carefully. Whenever we had these walks, it was always a learning experience. I mean, in so much as I learned a lot about him, and he learned about me. Now nearing the end of this walk, where one part of my life had ended with the breakup of my fiancée and me; and another part was beginning, I was sure Tony's words would be powerful. He looked at me and paused. The ball stopped moving and all was quiet. "I envy you," He said. I was silent, not even swallowing. I didn't know what to say. "You've dreamed things and done them! You're smart; you have many gifts, and you affect peoples' lives in a way that is amazing. I envy you." That's all he said; and that was enough. The rest of the walk we were silent…just kicking the ball back and forth. How would we break this tension that was now present? Neither knew what to say. Sometimes, when we don't know what to do, we go to our primordial instincts, and then sometimes, God knows just what you need when you need it. How many years had it been? How many adventures? We were still a team. It's kind of like a band. The members will change now and then, but the two founders always seem to stay with the band. From that first encounter many years ago, not much had changed.... Thank God! I don't remember how we ended the walk, or the talk for that matter. What I do know is that I felt better. Not because the situation had changed, but because I had not walked through it alone. Somehow our relationship had changed yet again. In the past, I had never really felt equal to him. It was nothing he did or said, but who he was and my own insecurity. In this conversation, he sealed for me my new confidence; my new outlook, and I would never be the same again.

2

From that first reunion at that Summer Recreation Program, Tony Scribble (Strubel) and I were pretty much joined at the hip. I got his phone number, he got mine, and we were in contact all the time. The program at the park lasted only until noon, so that kind of put a "hitch in our get-a-long," as my mother would say. That left us so much daylight, and yet we couldn't spend that time together, because I had to go home with my sisters.

Tony was an independent spirit. His parents both worked, and they trusted him (Mom and Dad Strubel, I know you're cringing even now as you read this years later.). Tony is a testimony to his parents though. I loved being at his house. I loved spending time with his parents. Not that my family wasn't a nice place to be, but the fact is that as Tony and I grew up, he was really an only child. Because of this, his parents were always genuinely interested in what we were up to, and really kinda gave us freedom to be kids. What better gift can you get. I'd walk in (without knocking) and his mom would be watching QVC, while his dad was out in the garden getting us the freshest tomatoes and squash in the land. I think I had more tomatoes growing up than any other kid. It spoils you though, when you have to eat that cardboard stuff all winter long. Long story short, though, it was a comfort place. His family dates back pretty far in the history of our small town, so everybody knew him. Whether his parents were at work or not, he had "surrogate" parents all over the place, so his parents trusted him a great deal.

The one thing we always talked about was a popular TV show at the time, known as *The A-team*. It consisted of four Vietnam Vets who become mercenaries and fight for the rights of the oppressed of society. Their claim to fame was their use of M-16 automatic rifles; but more characteristic was their creativity and ability to make the neatest gadgets and vehicles within a few hours. Now as children, of course we believed this could actually be done, and so began our plight as the new A-team, or the *B-team*.

The two of us identified well with certain characters on this show. Tony, as I mentioned previously, was "built" for a child his age, and so identified with the powerhouse, bully-type, with a negative attitude known as *B.A.* on the show. The character was played by "Mr. T" at the time, of "*Rocky III*" fame. Tony picked up on every part of this character, except for the attitude. That only came with time, and never developed to a negativity comparable to "Mr. T." I identified with two of the characters. I was by no means a leader, but I did have many ideas, plans, and schemes in my head, which kind of qualified me for the job. I identified with the boss who was known as "Hannibal," played very well at the time by George Peppard of *Breakfast at Tiffany's* fame. One of the other characters, Murdoch, (Dwight Schultz) was a crazy pilot, who was good for comic relief and flying; that was about it. I could identify, however, with his comic nature, and so went by his moniker most of the time.

Our group was a few members short, but that would come with time. We were ready to begin our "team." What we needed, is what every show began with that aired during those Tuesday nights in the eighties; a problem of oppression requiring a solution that only the A-team could solve. The show always began in the opening sequence with this quote: "If you have a problem that no one else can solve. And if you can find them. Then you can hire the A-team." Since we didn't have a problem… we made one up. We were typical imaginative kids.

Our problem began with a man named "Hattman". I don't even remember his first name. I do thank you though, Mr. Hattman, for providing two imaginative kids with a wonderful outlet during a summer break. Behind the diamond where we met, there was a cornfield. Beyond this cornfield was a company. This well-known company held its residence in Strasburg, up until about twenty years ago. As far as we were concerned, this company, up to the present anyway, had not done anything questionable with respect to the law. As far as we know now, they always did everything by the book, and did a great service to the public. That wouldn't have created much of an adventure for us, however, so back then we had to assume that this company was doing something illegal. I don't even remember now what we thought they were doing. (I know this is bad that I don't remember, but that is why I am writing this book now. I've waited long enough!) This is where Hattman comes in. Every episode of the A-team had one guy who was the ringleader, and usually at the end of the episode, had it out with Hannibal, who of course won. We too needed a ringleader and so we developed this guy, Hattman. I do believe it happened one day, when we saw a guy who appeared to be in charge. From that point on, he was thus deemed "Hattman."

Now that we had our "problem," we needed a base… a place that we could call our own. Currently, we had been hanging out in the cornfield or behind the baseball diamond. The recreation program ceased to exist for us on most days. We would arrive; check in; and then go down to the baseball diamond where I first encountered Tony. Then for the next three or four hours, we would just discuss, plan, and spy on anyone we saw outside of the building. *Ahhh, what a wonderful life!* Behind the diamond there were large sections of telephone poles, probably about five feet long, and a foot wide. There were also pieces of wood around, and piles of soil. We were ready to begin making our home base. This was our first "fort experience." There would be more.

Tony and I rolled the huge logs over to the area where the fort was to be built. We made a foundation from the logs that was about fifteen square feet. It was about three feet wide and five feet long. (I realize that this doesn't seem too large; however, to a child, anything is better than nothing.) We then slowly moved one of the logs on top of the other. Looking back those logs had to have weighed at least a hundred pounds, which goes to verify that Tony was much stronger than most kids his age. Even though we could get one log on top of the other, the log would roll on over the other side once released. There was no stability. We sat down and thought a moment about all the cabins we had ever seen and then realized what the problem was. There was nothing to hold the log in place. It just so happened that there was a water fountain behind the diamond, of the old stone type, which had a spigot at the base to hook up a hose.

As previously stated, Tony was the brawn, and I the brains. With my help, he did most of the moving of the logs, and I did more of the specifics, and fine-tuning. What fine-tuning, one might ask? As I said before, I was always coming up with these contraptions from my boundless imagination. I had discovered the wonderful world of levers even before I knew what they were, or what purpose they served. I had always seen in the movies and cartoons, how one would pull a lever and a trap door would open, or something would happen. And so construction began.

CHAPTER EIGHT

Home Base: The First of Many

1

Tomorrow was the day. I was going to be ordained a Deacon in the Roman Catholic Church: forever married to the Church. I would have no spouse or children of my own, but would devote my life to others. Tony and I had made a pact when we were younger. If he got married, which he did, I would be his "best man". And if I got married, he would be mine. The *best man* is responsible for the bachelor party, and other such details. Tony's bachelor party consisted of the two of us playing video games, talking shop, and discussing the future as we had many times before. We stayed up late and might have had a beer, but there were none of negative things that usually accompany such an event like strippers or drunkeness. We both knew that the next day would change our lives forever. It would not ever be the same again. It would never be so simple again. We never recalled any member of the "A-team" getting married, so this was uncharted territory. And we recalled a time when things were much simpler, and our greatest concern each day was how much sunlight we would have before having to retire for the evening.

This evening before my ordination was much the same as his bachelor party. He was my *best man*, for all times and places. He kept asking what he could do, and really there was nothing, other than providing the same service for me that I did for him. Therefore, the night before my ordination, he came over in the evening, and we took our last long walk. It reminded me of the long walk we had taken only years earlier when I had experienced the loss of my fiancee. He brought the ball, although, it had changed by now. It was slightly larger, (the size of a cantaloupe) and flat, so there was some control. We started at the corners of the usual haunt, we lit up our cigars and the games began. He looked at me and laughed. "With that cigar in your mouth you look like Hannibal Smith." I just quoted the character on the show: "I love it when…"

2

"…a plan comes together." The cement was working. We took the shovel and filled the wagon with some sand. Tony pulled the wagon over to the spigot, and filled the wagon with water. Using an old corn stalk, he mixed the sand and water, and vuela! We had cement. We were really rocking now. (No pun intended.) It was a cool summer morning; however, the humidity was high, and a haze settled over our small town. We rendezvoused at his house at about eight o'clock that morning. Our parents were already at work for the day, so it was up to my sisters to make it to the park on their own. This was not a bad walk or ride for anyone. It took about ten minutes to walk, on a bad day. Although Tony and I both had bikes, we chose to walk this particular day, because we had to bring along his red metal wagon. We went to his garage, the one that would later provide us with a fiery memory, and gathered all of the materials we "might" need. We placed all of the materials into the wagon, and began our walk down the bumpy sidewalk to what lay ahead of us at the park.

Tony and I arrived early that morning. Not even the counselors were there, which was fortunate for us. Sometimes I wondered if the counselors even knew who we were, or if they just dismissed us as "city kids" in the park. We entered the park and went directly back to the rear diamond, where all of our adventures occurred. As we parked the wagon carefully behind the back stop of the baseball diamond, we continued to discuss our plans for the day. We had to take care of our first priority and check on Hattman. We wanted to keep up with the surveillance, regardless of what our main objective was for the day. The corn was not yet as tall as we would have liked, but it was about five feet for the most part. More often than not, we ended up crawling on our bellies and elbows in order to avoid detection. The corn was definitely tall enough to hide two kids from any wandering eyes. After spying for awhile, our focus reverted to the creation of a fort. We began to plan the foundation of our fort, not on paper, but in our minds. First, we took the small shovel we had brought (pretty sad for a shovel actually), and began to smooth out the area that was to become the floor of our fort. There was a maple tree in the vicinity, and we decided to build the fort around the tree. The tree, in effect, would act as a watchtower, and would also be the control center as well. There were old stalks of corn lying around and plenty of sticks for supplies. With all these things at our fingertips, and a picture in our minds, construction began.

While Tony worked on our makeshift mortar, I had taken it as my personal mission to create the tower and control room. You never realize what things you actually should have brought with you to a project, until you need them and don't have them. We found this out over the next cycle of days. This particular day, however, I was up in the tree, and needed to clear branches. Because it was summer, our view was obscured by the leaves of this maple tree, and that presented certain problems; especially for a watchtower to perform the job for which it was created. Then we heard it!

I know that we heard it at about the same time, because we looked at each other and froze like rabbits at the sound of a coyote's cry. A low humming sound which brought to mind a small plane far off in the distance. This sound, however, was becoming louder by the second. Our eyes met, for the first time in a way that communicated more efficiently than words. From this point forward, Tony and I had reached a new level of understanding: a certain knowledge we had of each other that stemmed back to that first reunion here at the park. We would discover times when we could almost talk with our minds, just simply by giving a look. This particular look said *fear*. Not necessarily fear in the "scared sense", but fear in the sense that someone was about to discover our Eden. The B-team, the fort, and Hattman were all going up in smoke. I know to this day that he was thinking the same things. Should we run? Should we stand our ground? Where can we hide? What can we say? Then we saw it coming right for us. And the time for thinking was over. Now it was time to act.

A man on a large lawn mower was cutting the grass in the park before all of the kids would arrive, and he was heading right for us: the two of us caught red-handed with our "cement" filled wagon. The displaced logs were still in a makeshift rectangle. As the man approached, he lowered the throttle of the mower to a low hum. Our hearts started to race as he lumbered closer on his tractor. We continued to look on, and we noticed that he wasn't a man at all, *per se*, but a teenager, probably about sixteen or seventeen years old. When he finally reached us on the mower, he turned the key to the *off* position. The air was still…there was nothing but silence. His shirt was a mixture of dark and light gray splotches where the sweat had plastered his shirt to his body, and he was wearing a dark ball cap that must have been frying his head. He leaned back on the mower. "Hi boys. What's going on back here?" He tilted back his hat, as though it would release some of the steam from within his head, and as he did, I saw a change in Tony's eyes. They went from the look I had seen when we had our initial encounter at the beginning of the summer, to the look a person gets when they suddenly recognize someone. "Hersh!" Tony exclaimed, as though the mower man was a long lost puppy or something. The man, "Hersh," then replied, "Tony?" That was it. They obviously knew each other, and we were saved.

Tony walked up to the mower, but I held my ground in the tree. Hersh repeated his initial question, but without nearly as much authority as before. Tony had obviously known this guy for a long time growing up, and had not hesitated to approach him, once he positively identified him. "What are you guys up to?" "We're just 'hangin' out' back here," Tony replied. "We don't like the program, so we try to stay away from the barn where the counselors hang out." I was reading Hersh's body language, and it was saying that he didn't buy it. Not all of it anyway. He got up from the mower, and slowly walked toward me and the loosely formed foundation of logs. He looked up at me and said, "What's your name?" I told him my name was Mike, and that I was Tony's friend, hoping that he would say something to the tune of, "Any friend of Tony's is a friend of mine". I had to settle for just a smile instead. He began to circumspect the foundation. "What's all this stuff?" he asked. Tony jumped right in as if he had been cued by a prompter off-stage. "We're building a fort. We found this stuff laying around, and so we decided to put it to good use." I couldn't believe it. He told the truth! What was wrong with him. The first law of childhood is: "When you get caught red-handed, deny, deny, deny. If that doesn't work, *then* you can tell the truth." He had disobeyed the major law of kids everywhere. Hersh looked at us both, for what seemed like a lifetime, with a look of envy or nostalgia. "Cool. Well be careful, and don't get into trouble." That was all. The mower started up, and Hersh rode off into the sunrise.

That's it? No lectures about what we were doing? No turning us in to the proper authorities? What just happened here? Tony looked up at me with this smile (actually it was not a smile, but a grin). This was the first time I had seen this grin, but surely not the last. As he tilted his own hat back on his head, he remarked, "Hersh is cool". He was right. We began right where we had left off. I began to design the mechanisms, and Tony moved the logs. We were ready to try putting the second layer of logs on, so I descended the tree, and helped to lift. We got the log on top of the foundation log, and then I held it in place. Tony took his now partially solidified "cement", and began to pack it between the two logs with his hands. Looking back, I don't know what we were thinking. Science wasn't an understanding either of us had at the moment. After he had slapped all of this mud between the two, I released the top log. Tada! It stayed. It was time to try placing on another log. As the two of us were making our way to the second log, we heard a thump! and then a splotch. As we looked over, we saw our foundation log with mud on the top of it, and the log we had placed on top, laying outside of the foundation with mud on its underside. Back to the drawing board.

We repeated the process, however, this time we placed four corn stalks, two on either side of the top log, in an effort to brace it. The braces worked, and we decided that we would let the first log dry first, before attempting to stack another log on top. We worked well into the day. I was hammering nails through sticks and into the tree to make the necessary levers. Before we knew it, noon came and we had to get home. Although we had scarcely realized it at the time, during our effort to set the log back on top of the foundation, we inadvertently coated ourselves with mud. We were a mess. We gathered up all of the tools, which were also coated in our brown "cement" and made our way out of the park to Tony's house. There we hosed down everything, including ourselves, and went our separate ways, agreeing that tomorrow was another day, and yet another opportunity for adventure.

Needless to say, we were slightly "reamed out" for getting so muddy. That did not discourage us, however, but instead motivated us to be more careful in the future. (I'm sure that was really going to happen.) We met the next day at about the same time. It is amazing how early you can get up and how late you can go to bed when you're a kid, and yet the energy just keeps on coming. This day we were better prepared, because we loaded up the wagon, not only with the supplies we had taken yesterday, but also the stuff we didn't have yesterday, that we really needed. As was our custom now, we made our short trek to the park, discussing the whole way what plans were before us that day.

We arrived at the park, and as always, went into the field to see what was going on with Hattman. There was nothing to see this day, so we resumed construction where we had ended the previous day. Tony began to put on the second layer of logs, as I ascended the tree once more, in an effort to create the control tower.

My first mechanism I designed was for weapons. We had made little spears out of old corn stalks, with the assumption that if we were attacked, we could defend ourselves. (With cornstalks... yeah I know... I know.) The "spears" were balanced on one end by a branch on the tree, and on the other end by a small platform I had connected to the tree, on a pivot. A string was connected to the end of the platform, opposite the pivot. The other end of the string was connected to a lever. When I would pull the lever, the platform would drop, and the spears would subsequently drop, point first, to the ground. Ideally, we wanted them to drop and stick into the ground; however, we settled for them just dropping to the ground.

Now that the walls were beginning to form, we had an opening that would be our door. We strung the stalks and sticks together in order to make a door. Then I connected a string to the one end of the door, opposite its connection to the log wall, and the other end of the string to a lever in the control tower. When the person in the tower pulled the lever, the door would open up. This worked to a certain extent, but if you could imagine, corn stalks didn't make such a great door. It was home. At the end of the day, our fort was completed. It was only then that we noticed a third party making his way toward us on his bike. I saw him from our tower, and I pulled the lever for the weapons, which worked like a finely tuned machine. (Well… sort of.) The interloper approached, and as he did, Tony and I walked out from our domain to the bench running parallel to the diamond. We stood our ground.

As the boy approached, we relaxed a little bit. We observed that he was probably at least two years younger than we were. He had brown hair that was spiked up helter- skelter around his head, like a person who had been electrocuted and lived to tell the story. He looked intimidated, so at least we got the result we were looking for. He stopped the bike about ten feet from us, and just stood there sizing us up. Tony spoke first giving a basic "Hi." The boy responded with what appeared to be a bit of relief. "Wanna see what we're doing?" Tony asked. The kid's face lit up, and he replied, "Sure!" We had our new member.

I didn't know what to think at first, because I kind of liked the "dynamic duo", and was getting quite used to our particular roles. I never found out why Tony invited him in, but I assume it had to do with a few things. First of all, the kid was brave enough to approach us in the first place. That alone, was worth something. Two older guys (with spears) minding their own business, but with looks that could kill (or maybe maim at least). Secondly, the kid seemed innocent enough. He was like a lost puppy that needed some mentors. Lastly, and I do know this for a fact; Tony said for him to come back here like this, he must have been watching us for days. We had not discovered him spying on us, which was a discredit to us. A discredit to us, however, was a credit to him. We could use a surveillance guy who could go undetected, and a "go-fer" who could go back and forth between the park and us without being seen. Thus, we added "Face" to our group. The third member of the proverbial "A-team." We were almost complete. We had our problem to solve, our equipment, our "team," and our fort. We had all that we needed to be happy adventurers... or so we thought.

CHAPTER NINE

Creatures of the Night

1

I began to turn the corner in second gear and the engine protested with a high pitched hum that it wanted me to shift again. My arm was useless and my vision worsening with the tears and sweat in my eyes. I said to myself, "If I can just get to the pool, Tony's there and he'll be able to help". My wrist was badly broken, and there was nothing I could do. I had to shift, but it was my right wrist that was broken. I started the car and using my left hand, had shifted gears, but these were not straight roads. I released the clutch and shifted into third, laughing all the way and driving on the gray. My only thought was that if I could make it to the pool, I would be…

2

"Home Free." "Just like clock work. Everything according to the plan and we'll be *home free*." That was his line. I was doubtful. As we grow up and mature, (hopefully) we realize that some things we had once held sacred due to their obscure nature, become commonplace and almost boring in some sense. As a child, one fears the dark. Not so much because the "dark" itself can harm, or frighten, but the fact that we cannot see what is hiding in the dark. We are not able to perceive the creatures, ghosts, or other phenomena that use the darkness as a blanket to conceal their form, until it is too late. Kids… if we had only realized that the real boogie men are the ones who appear in movies and novels by Stephen King, we would have been able to focus our attention on the job at hand. Tony and I came to this realization early in life. The darkness held a fascination for the two of us, which was kind of ironic, considering all of the experiments we did with fire. Believe me when I tell you that neither of us liked to lose sleep over anything (and I believe we would agree, we still don't). In order to appease the drive within, however, we would have to go a step further than we had ever gone before. We would have to take a step we had not previously considered, and had we known all of the doors this step would open to experience, we probably would have made it much sooner… or maybe not at all.

The two of us sat in my room and watched the clock. The digital face read 11:26 PM. We weren't talking too much, just sitting there trying to keep our eyes open. Every now and then I would say to Tony, "I'm just resting my eyes," to which he would respond, "Well get'em open, we can't afford to fall asleep. We've waited much too long and we can't fail this mission tonight." He was right. We had tried two other weekends to stay up until the designated time, and failed miserably both times. Probably at least one of those times was due to "resting my eyes." We had been planning this night for weeks, talking sometimes casually about it, and other times describing in great depth what we were undertaking and how we were to accomplish this mission. There was no room for fear or laziness here. It was tonight; or never.

The basic plan was a night walk. We wanted to get out of my parents' house, walk around town, and return undetected. Simple enough, right? Well not exactly. These things had to be planned very delicately. And so we began to conspire how we would stay up; get out of the house undetected, and get back without getting caught. That was the clincher. What if we *did* get caught? Well, to put it bluntly, our current life as we knew it, would end. I know that I would have been grounded, and my parents would have looked at Tony as a bad influence. We had to look at every conceivable outcome, and take many precautions. This would, and did, take considerable planning.

I was beginning to rest my eyes again. The digital clock now read 11:45 PM. It was getting closer to the time. "What are we gonna do if we get caught?" I said this for two reasons that I can now think of. The first was that I had to talk. It was too quiet, and I was falling asleep, as I'm sure he would also do shortly. The second reason was that I really wanted to review the plans we had made... just in case. "Remember, if we get caught outside, we split up and regroup at my garage. We can plan from there." "So to get out, we leave by the front door? What about my dog?" Tony said, "That's where you come in. You know how to open that door without making it creak. It has to be quick. We already know it can't be opened slowly. We only get one chance at this. If we get caught inside, our cover is blown."

In many respects, it was on my shoulders this time. The front door to our house was a heavy metal door that stuck tight in the door frame, and squeaked when opened slowly. It's funny how you never notice these things during the day, when it doesn't really matter. After Tony finished briefing me, he took out the plans and went over them. "We will go out the front door, and proceed to the cars in the driveway. When it's clear, I'll go across the street. When it's safe, I'll signal you to come over and join me." I understood what he said, and was kind of glad to hear the plans again. My hard part was the inside; once we were out, it was all Tony's ball game.

It was now 12:01 AM. We had to make sure everyone was in bed. To go out before everyone was asleep (including the dog) would be a grave mistake…a mistake that we probably would not get an opportunity to repeat. We had decided that the ETD, or *estimated time of departure*, was to be 12:30AM. The last week, we had made it to about 12:15 and then fell asleep. I was now getting my second wind, and we were both nervous. There was no chance of falling asleep now. The adrenaline was flowing.

At 12:20AM, we began to get dressed. I wore black sweatpants with a black tee-shirt. My sneakers were white, so I put black socks over my sneakers. Tony wore black sweats, a dark shirt, and of course his captain's hat. We were both armed with dart guns and pocket knives, for who knew what danger we might encounter. We were ready to go. We both sat facing each other as though we might be heading out for the last time. No one spoke, but the whole time I was praying, "Please Lord don't let us get caught". The Lord answered my prayer that night; not in the way I would have liked, but He did answer it, indeed.

I was located in a room on the second floor. My room was on the left front side of the house. The only room with no roof awning outside of the window on which to step. Was this a factor? Not tonight, but in future nights it would be. Because there was no other way out, we had decided to go out the front door of the house. The front door was pretty well lit, as was the porch, so we would have to be quick.

The clock downstairs gave two chimes, so we knew the hour had come. We checked each other to make sure our equipment was ready, and as I looked at Tony's face, and he at mine, I believe we were both thinking the same thing. We were both thinking of not going through with it; of giving up the opportunity that we might never get again.

And for that split second, I believe we were both ready to sit back down, get undressed, and go to bed. At the moment, I started back towards the bed; however, Tony put out his hand and grabbed the door knob to my bedroom; and with that simple twist, there was no turning back… we were gone.

He opened my bedroom door and softly crept down the carpeted stairs. As we reached about the middle of the stairs a board creaked for what seemed to be an eternity. We just started giggling, in a silent breathless laugh. Was this really the time for hysterics?! It didn't matter. A good bit of nerves rode out on that laughter. Tony, composed himself, looked back at me and whispered: "We'll have to watch that one on the way back." For the first time, I had a warm feeling inside. This feeling said that we were coming back. I hadn't really thought about what would happen after we got outside and did what we went out to do. I never thought how we would get back safe and sound. I guess I just never saw that far into the future.

I continued down the steps, careful not to tread on the same board that Tony had, but all the while my mind was in a different place. I was no longer in my house, and sneaking out, but was living the *mission*. We reached the bottom of the staircase, and our sock-clad sneakers slid across the blue-stone colored linoleum. Tony stepped back, as though I were diffusing a bomb, or getting ready to trip a mine. He watched and waited as I did my "magic". I grabbed the door knob with my right hand and put my thumb on the button in the middle of it. I braced my left hand on the jamb and door and applied pressure. I slowly turned the doorknob, and as I did, I felt the little push button lock give, and the door made a pop. The door was so tightly sealed in the door frame, that when we shut it at night (or any time for that matter), we would have to put our weight against it, and push until it clicked. When we would turn the knob then, the door would spring out from the door frame like a Jack-in-the-box, and usually let out a loud pop. This night, unfortunately, was no exception.

We froze, like rabbits in the midst of a predator. We froze and listened. We must have stood there for about two minutes, all the while breathing rapidly and sweating; our hearts pounding like jack hammers. This was the tough part now. If the dog heard the door, her natural instinct would be to bark. From that, my parents' natural instinct was to wake up and find out what the dog was barking at; and thus a chain reaction that would not be beneficial to us in the least bit. I grabbed the knob with both hands, and looked back at Tony. His eyes were stone. He was calm and focused, and that is what I think gave me the strength to do what I did next. He had full faith that I would pull this off without a hitch, and that faith gave me the courage and confidence to do just that. With a quick tug, I pulled the door open to about half of its capacity, or about two feet. The door let out a muffled squeak, that was barely audible. The first part was over. The next part was to get the door closed again, once we exited, without locking ourselves out.

Tony moved into position and opened the storm door as I had the heavy door. We quickly moved through the opening, and I tugged the front door without a thought, pulling it just enough to make it look shut to an outsider. We skittered over to the cars in the driveway and could barely contain ourselves. WE MADE IT! We had done it! All the planning had paid off; however, it was all for naught if we didn't get through our mission and get back undetected. This was going to take some skill, and brains. It was a good thing that we had a little bit of both.

The first mission was a rescue mission. Over the last few days we had seen a cat in the basement of the house across the street. Whenever we were near, it would jump to the basement window, and paw at the glass, as though it were trapped. We had decided that it was, indeed, being held against its will, and so decided that it was up to us to rescue the helpless beast. We crouched in between the two cars (one was a van) and tried to calm down. We both looked at each other, and our smiles said it all. Tony gave me a quick look as if saying: "Do you remember the plan?". I returned his gaze and gave a quick nod of affirmation. He scanned the house across the street in an effort to find where he would go next. As he did, I scanned the street in both directions. Situated in front of my house was a street light. That night it might as well have been a spotlight. That was our main obstacle right now.

Before I finished my second glance down the street, Tony was gone. He whipped across the street just as headlights broke over the horizon. The car was moving at a reasonable pace for the suburbs, and Tony dove behind a bush on the other side of the street. I crouched behind the van, and as the car approached, moved in an effort to always have a car between me and those headlights. This particular night, the car didn't only have headlights, but also had police lights on top! It was our Township police car, and it was slowing down.

As the car approached, I swallowed hard. My heart once again began to thunder as if it were a snare drum at a percussion competition. My first instinct was to run, but running was not an option... not with Tony across the street. The plan flashed through my head: "We split up if we get caught, and meet back at my garage." I couldn't leave Tony there though. So many things flashed through my head at once. We had done it... and in doing so... we were past the point of no return.

I saw a dark shade crouching behind the last bush in front of the neighbor's house. Certainly the cop hadn't seen Tony cross the street. By the time the headlights had broken over the horizon, he was safely in hiding. But these cruisers had spotlights as well, and if per chance a white sock, or blond head poked out from behind the bush, the officer would certainly see him, and Tony would be trapped. The police car now slowed considerably, and I was really starting to sweat. Tony was motionless, and had I not known where he ran to, I would never have spotted him in the darkness. I think in retrospect, that because the cop had not seen where Tony ran to, he didn't see anything out of the ordinary.

As the cruiser accelerated and passed the house, I thanked God that he had come through with His end of the bargain… up to this point at least. Tony stood up from the bush, ensured that the coast was now clear, and ran the back side of his right forearm across his forehead as if to say, "That was a close one". He didn't know how right he was. We scanned the streets twice this time, and then I bolted across the street, and met with him at his current position. The moon was not full this night, but was bright enough to provide us with light.

We were at the target house, but didn't see the cat. There were six basement windows, so we had to search all six, just in case there were different rooms in the basement. We searched the two side windows and then went to the back of the house. "Shhh." Tony said. "Listen." I didn't hear anything, but waited silently. "Hear that?" Tony said. And this time I did hear something; but what? It sounded like a chain dragging on the ground. It could very well have been the wind blowing something around, or a flag pole with a blowing rope; however, that was not the case. We listened again, and this time the muffled clattering of the chain was followed by a low growl. Growl! We both looked at each other instantaneously and mouthed "Tasha!" As we mouthed her name, we turned around, and now the growls and clinking were followed by some white teeth belonging to a German Shepherd. So it began.

We both froze, as we had earlier that evening. We had considered many consequences of sneaking out. We thought that we might at some point get caught… we just never considered that it would be anything other than a human that would catch us. We just stared at her, and if our eyes could have spoken, they would have said, "Please Tasha, of all the times, don't bark now". Tasha was the gentlest old dog you would ever want to know. Right now, though, she didn't know who we were; and that was dangerous. Maybe if we could get closer, she would recognize us, and then jump us with a wagging tail, and a sloppy kiss for each. The problem was that Tasha was old, and her sight wasn't what it used to be. Be that as it may, we cautiously approached in the hope that if she didn't recognize us by sight, she would certainly recognize our scent.

We both began to walk slowly, and Tasha didn't wait for the second step before she began to bark, very loudly and incessantly. Her teeth were gleaming in the moonlight, and she gave us everything she had. The barks were deep, and gruff, and one could tell she had used that bark well over the years. You could hear the age in that bark, but at this point, the timbre of the bark didn't matter much, it was the volume that was all too effective. Without a second's hesitation we bolted across the street. There was not clearance or surveying for cars involved, we just ran. We finally stopped behind the van in my driveway, and looked for lights to go on at her master's house. She was still barking, but it was now an exhaustive bark, as if she was finally out of breath. No lights came on at the master's house. We looked at one another, and knew that the mission was over. We had acted prematurely and carelessly, and now risked getting caught... a risk that neither of us could afford. I took the socks off of my sneakers, and asked a rhetorical question. I say the question was rhetorical because I knew the answer, and also knew that Tony was upset, and wouldn't respond in all probability. "Well, is that it? Are we done?" We headed for the front door, a little less stealthily, and with a little less adrenaline flowing.

We had made it out for only a few minutes, but if we messed up here, that would be the end for both of us... at least for a while. Tony yielded to me, and I checked the front door. It was just as I had left it. I placed my left hand firmly on the door, as if I were testing to see how hot it was, and placed my right firmly around the bronze knob. Tony held the screen door in place, and in one swift movement, I opened the door to about half its capacity. We paused and listened. No sound came from anywhere, so I entered the foyer, and Tony followed. I turned and grasped the knob again, and was prepared to close the door when I heard a bark! My innocent little dog, sleeping in my parents' room let out one loud bark. We were frozen. If I continued to close the door, she would certainly hear the sound, and begin barking frantically. If we didn't close the door, chances were we would be caught, if not by my parents, by the cruiser that was making its way back up my street. The cruiser was slowly moving around the corner and the lights were about to hit our front door. I didn't have to make the decision, Tony said "Close it!" under his breath, gruffly, and as I closed the door, the headlights of the cruiser skimmed across the white front of the door, and reflected off of our eyes.

As expected, another bark came from the room, followed by a low growl. Now my dog wasn't all that ferocious, but it wasn't her ferocity we were concerned with---it was her volume and the ability to rouse people from sleep. As I was pressurizing the door to get it to click, we heard my dad say "Hush!" to the dog. In a moment, we also heard the mattress in the room creaking. My dad was getting up, and we were as good as caught. There were three entrances into the foyer. The first was from the hallway leading to my parents' room. The second was the front door. The third was a door way to the living room. There was no door at this entrance, but only an open arch. We could not run upstairs, for my dad would certainly hear us on those wooden stairs, so we did the next best thing.

We heard my dad's room door open, and the jingling of the dog's tags on her collar. As he reached the door to the foyer from the hallway, and turned the knob, we swiftly moved into the living room. We were still dressed in our dark clothes, but didn't think of this at the time. We then heard the front door make that boom sound, and my dad creaked the door open. As soon as we heard him let the dog out on the leash, we went into the kitchen. This is where improvisation took place. Tony got out two bowls, and "Smurf-berry Crunch" a popular cereal at the time. We both sat down at the table and began to eat. It was dry, but it didn't matter. We also had a bag of chips there that we were downing. Sweat was pouring off of our faces, and our hearts were beating wildly. We heard the dog come back in, and were prepared for whatever lay ahead for us. My dad walked through the foyer door, back into the hallway. When he spied us in the dim kitchen light, he jumped with a slight "Oh". The dog came over to us and was sniffing at our feet. Thus began the inquisition.

We both looked up at him, as innocent as two teenage boys can look, and said: "We were hungry, so we came down for a snack." My dad wears thick prescription glasses, and so was squinting a bit without them, but didn't take much note of our clothes. "I thought I locked that front door before I went to bed." Both Tony and I stopped in mid crunch of our cereal. Silence fell heavily on the room, and I believe even the dog was looking at us, as if to say, "What are you gonna say now boys?" He walked back out toward the front door and made sure the door was locked. Thoughts were flashing through our minds as to whether we may have tracked in mud, or dirt. Had we covered all of our bases? He slowly returned to the kitchen as though he were running through the evening's events in his mind, still uncertain of whether he had locked the door before going to bed, or not. He turned toward us, and stared for a moment, and then said, "Good night boys. Turn off the kitchen light when you go to bed." That was it.

We quickly finished our cereal, and took the box upstairs with us. There was no cautious creeping this time; we ran up the steps. As soon as we closed my room door, our laughter released like a flood gate. It was a mad sort of laughter, as one who has just escaped fate laughs until he cries. All we did for the next hour was recap to each other our encounter with my father, and how close we had come to getting caught. Inevitably, though, we fell asleep, and only the following day did we begin to analyze our mistakes, under a daylight sun. Who knows what would have happened had we been caught. What I do know, is the fact that we didn't get caught that particular night, paved the way for future escapades, which would surely lead to further adventures, for creatures of the night.

CHAPTER TEN

The End... and New Beginnings

1

Those summer days were the most memorable times of my life for two reasons: The first reason was that I had run back into Tony after so many years, and together, we had built a fort and a "team". The other reason was the adventure, which was our life. During the day, we were out and about, but we were no longer limited by the night. The night and darkness was our friend. The "team" was a daily presence at the park now. We spied on the other kids while they did their activities, and of course kept tabs on Hattman and all of his "activities." Our third member "Face" was doing his part to bring us information, or whatever else we needed from the outside. We were living life to the fullest. At the end of the week, however, our adventure came to an abrupt end.

2

We arrived at the park late one day, which presented some problems in getting back to the fort, without being detected. We had ridden our bikes, and so we coasted up and down the path close to the baseball diamond. We did this for about fifteen minutes until we were no longer an object of focus for counselors, and then made a mad dash toward the area of our fort. Upon arrival, we were speechless. The levers and platforms on the tree had been torn down. The strings, used to mechanize the weapons and door, were dangling lifelessly at the ends of the branches like tinsel on a Christmas tree branch. The sticks had been broken, and the nails removed from the tree. The logs that had been so carefully placed one on top of another, were scattered, as though some one had mindlessly torn though our creation. The spears were tossed in the field beside where the fort used to stand. There was only one question on our minds: "Who?"

Of course our first conclusion was that Hattman had something to do with it, however, even in our prepubescent minds we knew that Hattman had nothing at all to do with this. This vicious act was done by someone who knew; someone who knew we were back here, and building a fort. This was done by someone who would have done this after we had left at noon. We both looked at "Face" and immediately sent him out to find out what he could. He went as if he had the most important mission in the world that day. And thinking back, I guess that day, he did.

We had an important decision to make. Tony and I sat down and began to discuss our future. We could either rebuild and try to guard the fort, or we could scrap the whole idea. We weighed our options, costs and benefits, but eventually, we decided to rebuild, and so the process began again. Face returned with no information at all, but said he would keep watch throughout the day "undercover" to see if anyone was spying on us.

About this time, a fourth party was approaching us. We had nothing to hide at this point, because we had no fort. This fourth party also was quite different from the three of us, in that "she" was a girl. As she got closer to where we were, once again Tony got a look of recognition in his eyes. Was there anyone this guy *didn't* know? "Katrina," he said with a whisper I think he only intended for himself to hear. Katrina was a short, thin girl who had been friends with Tony since they were toddlers. This short thin girl seemed fairly harmless until she opened her mouth. She had a tongue that was sharp as a knife, and took no grief from us at all. She was the attitude we were looking for, that Tony never picked up for himself. The A-team had a woman who would help them on the outside, and get them out of sticky situations from time to time. Katrina was now our "Amy."

With the help of "Amy," and "Face" we began to rebuild our fort. The gears were different, and better than before, and Tony was learning how to make stronger walls as well. This fort would be better than the first.

The next day, the "Team" convened at the barn, at eight o'clock as agreed. We filled "Amy" in on Hattman, and what was going on. Once she had been briefed and sworn to secrecy, we headed to the fort. For the second time that week, we were speechless. Once again, the walls were in ruins, and the levers had been torn from the tree. No strings remained, so whoever did this, took them this time. For the first time, I heard Tony swear. But I almost laughed when, after he swore, I heard him say: "Sorry dear Lord". That has stayed with me, even to this day.

That was it. We were defeated by some unseen demon who was determined to keep us down. Who could it have been? Just then, we heard that hum that was so familiar, and yet still struck a bit of fear in us. It was Hersh. Amy and Face jumped up, ready to run, until Tony assured them that Hersh would do us no harm. As Hersh approached on the mower, once again, he lowered the throttle to a low murmur. He didn't turn off the engine this time, but hopped off the mower. It was cooler today, so he wasn't sweating nearly as much as last time. "What's going on guys?" he said. Then something "clicked". Tony looked up at him with weary eyes. Tony knew who did this. "Someone destroyed our fort," Tony said. He could tell by the look on Hersh's face, that we had found our man. "I thought you guys were just hangin' out back here. You didn't say anything about putting nails in the tree." Tony looked at him as though he had been stabbed in the back. "You didn't have to destroy our fort; you just had to tell us not to put nails in the tree," Tony said. "Sorry guys, I'm just doing my job. You can't be back here anymore." With that he got back on the mower, and rode off, as he had, not two weeks before.

We were all silent. How quickly the membership of the team had increased, and how quickly it had been disbanded. We had to talk. We had to decide what we were going to do. If we were to disband, would that mean Tony and I would also disband? If we built another fort, we couldn't build it here. At that moment, we heard a helicopter, and it sounded really low to the ground. As imaginations often do, ours went wild. We assumed that this was Hattman's helicopter, and that they too, had seen us spying on them. We ran, but didn't run toward the park. We ran parallel to the corn field and then into brush. We made it to the other side of the brush, and found a pine forest. It was filled with beautiful trees, which had grown so close together that their lower branches received no light, and so were dead. We had a canopy of pine branches with a wide-open area underneath. We now had our new hideout for the time being. It was a forest, and thus we deemed it "The Enchanted Forest." We were a team once again.

CHAPTER ELEVEN

New Discovery: The World of Girls

1

We walked down the first block, just kicking that ball back and forth. A woman came out and began to line up her garbage cans on the street. She knew us, because we had been friends with her daughters so many years ago, and let's face it: everybody knew everybody, more or less.

2

It's different growing up in a small town. Our town was a wonderful piece of *Americana* right here in the East. And in the "Eighties"…well, it was just a slice of heaven. I'm sure there were troubles in our town; I'm sure there were secrets and black smudges on our moral record somewhere or another, but it was a wonderful place to grow up. That is, before it became the tourist area that it is now; before they tried to cram so many *clone* houses into it; before the outlets; before the tours, it was our town. It was our home. What a dream! You don't realize how really good it is, until it's not the same as it was anymore.

The Strasburg pool was where everybody went in the summer, even though it only took "members." Tony made a career out of that place, and if he wasn't at home, he was there for the most part. The pond next to it, was one of my favorite places on the earth and even now holds many fond memories for us. It was a sacred place. We dug our first underground fort there; I had a romantic dinner date there for a lovely girl named Monica. We fished there; we swam there (until the cruisers showed up); it was a dream. A few miles down that same street were the caves, where we would spend hours on end, both in summer and winter. And if you continued past the pool for a few miles, there was Little Beaver Creek, where I broke my wrist, and where we began to build another underground lair. Next to the pool was the elementary school, where I attended kindergarten, and the obstacle course on which we trained. We would head down to "Pizza City" to see Sam, get some lunch and maybe some advice on life. There was the bowling alley, where we spent countless hours shoving quarters into video games and shooting pool. I remember many of the seedy characters who shot pool, and they inspired me…not to be like them. We weren't terribly good at pool; at least not as good as they were, but we were a lot better at life, and that's what mattered most. On down from the bowling alley was a "Turkey Hill" convenience store, where we would get a cigar now and then, or a *MAD* magazine. This was our world, and what a world it was.

3

We wanted to continue our stroll, but as she finished lining up the cans on the sidewalk she took a few seconds to embrace us, and ask how we were. We remembered this house fondly, for it was a frequent stop on our night walks in days past. Times had changed a little that summer, as I remember. I couldn't put my finger on it at the time, but I think in retrospect I know exactly what it was. We began to grow up.

4

Up to this time, Tony and I worked as a team. It was just the two of us, and that is how we liked it. We had gone through that "A-team" stage, and of course Katrina would always be with us (little did I know I would take her to her senior prom). But at this stage of the game, I began to notice something different about Tony. He was starting to spend a lot of time around girls. Now Tony was built to begin with, but as he got into middle school, and started wrestling and playing football, he began to develop his body in a way that made it look proportional, and at the same time disciplined. He was a rock, and had some handsome features to boot. It might be more correct to say that the girls were hanging around him more than they used to. He didn't much complain about this; however, and so I will assume that it was a mutual thing. As much as the girls hung around him, he never let them distract "him" from the "us." We were still a team, and no girl would ever come between us... at least not until later.

We continued to sneak out of the house; however, we became more adept at it, and it became no more than a small formality to our freedom. We modified the escape route slightly, however. We began to escape through the upstairs bathroom window. This was a bit risky due to the fact that we were upstairs, and would have to walk across the roof, which of course, would make some noise. This method proved most effective, however, and so we employed it for the remainder of our nightly escapades. We would climb out on the roof, walk silently to the edge and then on "three" jump off into freedom. (See, I knew I would get to fly.) We would land on the ground, tuck and roll, and then continue a short sprint to the corner hemlock and wait to see if lights went on. If the house remained dark (and it always did), we would commence with the activities for the evening. I should note here, that Tony got caught only once. The only time he went out with my brother Joe instead of me, and they walked down to the neighbor girls who were sleeping out in a tent, they got caught. All they remember is hearing that upstairs bathroom window slam shut and lock…but I digress.

Tony had gotten to know quite a few girls, our age, thus our missions began to change slightly. This particular night Tony was staying over, we decided that we would visit the house of one of these girls. Her parents were away for the weekend, so this would not be a problem. We had no problem staying up that night, because it was the first time we had ever done anything like this. It was certainly the first time I had. I was what you call a "late bloomer". I matured later than Tony did, for whatever reason. I was not interested in girls until about my early to mid teens, and certainly did not possess the confidence to approach a girl, unless I knew her pretty well. The problem I dealt with, on a daily basis, was that I went to the city school, but lived in the country. Most of the kids in the neighborhood went to Tony's school, so he knew them. That was an advantage I lacked. The people I did know from L-S, I knew only through Tony.

This particular night we had waited until one o'clock AM. We were having no problem staying awake, so we figured it would be better to be safe than sorry. This was only about our fourth time out, and only our second time through the window. We crept out of my room, and went to all of the other rooms upstairs and pulled their doors shut, so not to disturb anyone. We went into the bathroom, and closed the door. This bathroom window was smaller than the windows in the bedrooms, and was higher up on the wall. The bathtub ran the length of the wall to the right as you entered the bathroom, and then to the left of the tub and about four feet off the floor was the window. Tony got the lights, and slowly, I opened the window and then the screen. We could feel the brisk night air flow through the window, as if it had been waiting to be let in. I went out the window first, planting my right foot on the rim of the tub, and carefully maneuvering my left leg through the open window, until I felt solid shingles under my foot. I then ducked and pulled my head and right leg through.

Our blood began to heat up, and we got those proverbial butterflies in our stomachs. That was the rush I suppose. Tony repeated my maneuver through the window, and then carefully shut it. He then pulled down the screen until there was about an inch of clearance. We walked as close to the outer wall of the house as possible, and made our way over to the chimney, where we sat down on the edge of the roof, and with a quick glance at each other, we planted our hands, and pushed ourselves over the edge. We landed with a tuck and roll and scurried quickly for cover, as we waited to see which, if any, lights would come on. In retrospect, I really don't know why we waited. If a light did go on, we were stuck.

From our safe zone, we made our way up through my back yard and toward the target house. We saw flashes coming from the house, and so we surmised that the girls were watching TV; however, we were cautious. Nothing would be worse than to knock on a window, and have a parent come to the door. We spied through the window, and as we expected, the two were there watching TV. Tony knocked on the window and the *butterflies* began to flutter again.

A thousand and one thoughts went through my head at that moment. What was I getting into here? I was fourteen years old, and a "good kid" relatively speaking. What was I doing going into someone else's house, at one in the morning, where two girls were waiting alone for two guys to come and visit? Hello? Is there anyone thinking here?! The room got quiet after Tony knocked, and a little giggling emanated from the room. The curtain pulled back just enough that we could see an eye peeking out, and then we heard the click of the door. We were in. They were watching a movie, and had been lying on the floor on sleeping bags, as was the classic scenario at sleepovers. Tony and I seated ourselves on the sofa, and he began to talk, "small talk". It was quite obvious to me that we were all uncomfortable. Lord knows I was. I was very insecure at this age, so I pretty much kept to myself, as I sat there watching Tony lull these ladies with his soliloquy.

As I sat pondering all of our insecurities, a beer was produced. Now I had had sips of beer from my Granny when I was younger, and I didn't like the taste then. Tony had a sip, as did the two girls, so I was the only one left. I took a sip, and tried to hide my disgust. I don't know how I got that gulp down, but I managed to stomach it, and that was all I had the rest of the night. I didn't have to worry though, because the other three didn't seem to mind the awful taste, so before too long the beer was out of sight, and out of mind.

Now Tony had, what I call his "honey speak." The reason I called it that, was that it was sickening sweet like honey, and as thick as horse manure, but the girls loved it. In fact, the only girl to this day, I believe, that could always see through this stuff, is now his wife, Missy. I also think that is why he married her. This ability to see through his façade is what made her special. And to this day she still sees through his manure, on a daily basis. But I digress. His "honey speak," was his way of warming up to the ladies, and essentially enamoring them. He began the lulling and before too long, he was sitting on one of the girls' backs as she lay on her belly, and giving her a shoulder rub. Now there was no therapeutic value in this whatsoever; however, it was the physical contact that was important here. At this, I just sat on the sofa, afraid to move. I didn't even want to acknowledge that there was anyone else in the room. What was I doing here? Which of these things did not belong? Me!

5

I sit back and try to recall the memories of us together during our actual "dating years." Tony and I never went on a "double date". We only went to one prom together at which neither danced unless the song had a beat that necessitated a partner. I got to know all of Tony's girlfriends, and then again really not. It seemed that when we were together, for the most part, that it was just us. And the things we spoke of when it was just "us" were not girls. Unique when you think about it. I'm not saying that when we went down to the shore that we had custody of the eyes necessarily, but that our relationships; our dates; our love spats with our significant other, never seemed to make the top ten list when it came to our palavers. The irony is that much later, the ladies in our life would be at the center of our discussions; our plans; and later on, even our disagreements.

6

I felt like just getting up and leaving, but what would I do? At this time, the other girl complained that Tony was ignoring her, leaving him with no choice but to switch his attention to her. What is humorous, in retrospect, is the fact that this is all that occurred for the next hour or so. There was no kissing, or hugging, or any "fooling around," but simple attention. Attention from a guy by whom these girls were obviously smitten.

Tony must have sensed my discomfort, because he began his farewell speech. We certainly did share a mind between us, and he knew that I didn't belong in this situation. We realized this night, how different the two of us really were. It had never occurred to us, because we were always exclusive to our personalities when we were together. I never saw him at school, or at games, etc. nor did he see me. It was certainly a learning experience. This night changed our roles in a significant way.

Our roles were no longer defined by external features like intelligence or strength, but by our morals and personalities. No longer was I necessarily characterized as the intelligent one, but the one who was a "good boy." That is not to say that Tony was bad, but is to say that he grew up in a different environment, and for the environment in which he grew up, he was the norm. He, therefore, was characterized as the "bad boy." I'm not going to discuss the things he did to characterize him like that. He can tell you that if he decides to write his book (Yes Tony... That book!) but we had gone through a rite of passage this night. For the first time, we saw each other in a tested environment. We both passed the test; however, in passing we came to know another side of each other, and one that we would come to love in each other.

We returned to my house that night. We climbed up the bricks of the chimney, which was no great feat for Tony, but which required me to stand on a trash can to reach. We maneuvered back through the bathroom window, but not carefully enough. As I planted my boot through the window, it landed on the towel rack underneath and knocked it against the porcelain tub and onto the floor. I froze. Tony yelled "GO!" If anyone heard the rack hit, we were dead. I don't think Tony touched the sill as he hurled through the window, quickly replacing the screen and dropping the window frame. I picked up the towel rack and carefully hitched it up on the mount. It looked...well... semi-normal. I put a small wash cloth over it as a finishing touch and we scurried back into my room.

No one came upstairs, and although I did feel a little guilty the next morning when my sister pulled the towel off and we heard the rack hit the ground, we were not suspected. We didn't talk much about the night probably because we were both tired, and trying to process it all in our heads. I didn't fall asleep for quite awhile. I was thinking about what happened tonight... about how I felt being there with the girls. I was not particularly attracted to either of them, but somehow the fact that we had so easily pulled it off, didn't seem quite right. I guess I felt cheated somewhat, because there was really no challenge to tonight's adventure. The focus had changed, and so I wondered what the future held for us. Whether these nightly visits would become the rule, or whether it was simply a once and done thing. I heard Tony breathing slowly and deeply, so I knew he had finally fallen asleep. I would find that this was only the first in a series of nightly visits to different houses, few of which we would enter. The ones following this one were different somehow. And it was only later that I determined what the difference was… the girls were becoming interested in me.

CHAPTER TWELVE

Of Love and Loss

1

As I said before, I was a bit of a late bloomer. I wasn't interested in girls, or at least not interested in the risks of approaching them at least until high school. I still had this insecurity, and didn't think myself that attractive in the least. Tony was the one with all the girls, and I remember having various conversations with him about this. "But how do you say it?" "You know…just talk to 'em boy. Don't be intimidated by them. Man! Why are you so scared?" "I don't know what it is…it just doesn't feel right." That was true, but it was also the *interest factor*. I just didn't see the point. The girls seemed all giddy. I had spent a great part of my summer at the pool. I had begun working nights at the golf course, so I could spend my days at the pool. As a result, I got to know many of Tony's friends, some of whom then became my friends. There were these girls who were also beginning to hover around me. I couldn't put my finger on it. Why were they so interested? Tony told me it was because I was so shy, and they thought that was cute. "Great…so I'm

cute. A puppy is cute…a teddy bear is cute. I don't want to be cute."
He would just laugh.

One of these girls, I had been with in kindergarten. Who would've
thought after all this time we would reconnect. But that was our town:
"Small-town USA". Well, it came to pass that this girl was having a
sleep-over. At the sleep-over would be her and her friend. I think Tony
was interested in her friend, but really, who could tell. The plan was
simple. We were going to sneak out of the house again and go visit these
girls. "Why are we going to do this?" "Because we can," he retorted.
Then he paused a moment. He looked right at me and said: "Listen;
you said you wanted to be more confident. You said you wanted to feel
comfortable. Here's a girl who's interested in you! Here's your chance.
This isn't the first time we've done this, I mean come on already." "But
Tony, it *is* the first time we've been out with your peg-leg." Tony had
Osgood Schlatter disease. I used to call it "Ostrich Slaughter." This was
a disease that affected his knee. He was in an immobilizer from the
thigh to the shin. He had to keep the leg straight when he walked. And
we were supposed to sneak out under these circumstances? Yeah right!

The clock read 1:30 AM. We had waited extra late and were getting
better at staying up. *Super – C* and *Mega-man 3* helped in the effort.
In fact, sometimes we were so fixated on beating the game, that we
decided not to sneak out at all, but just to stay in and play. Because of
Tony's leg, we had to leave by the back porch door. This was a sliding
glass door, which was much quieter than the front door, but less stealthy
than the window. We did leave the window unlocked in the event the
back door got locked. Even though the porch door was glass and slid
soundlessly, the porch screen door was like most others. It had a rusty
spring which sounded at the slightest extension, and a clasp on the
outside which would snap when you least expected. Having cleared the
first security center without having been detected, we made our way
through the backyard and into the night.

I felt the way I did the first time we had gone out in the night. Not because we were sneaking out, but because of the destination. Why were we even doing this? I mean really, what were we going to do? "So what's gonna happen when we get there?" I asked. "What do you mean?" "Oh man, you remember that night with the two girls and the beer? Can you say awkward boys and girls?" Tony let a laugh escape. "We'll just go with the flow. We're just going to go in and hang out for a little while, that's all." I still didn't see the purpose of the whole thing, but I had his back. "Where are her parents? Are they away for the week or what?" "Her parents are upstairs sleeping I imagine. What are you so nervous about?" "Upstairs sleeping! Are you kidding me! So let me get this straight: we're going into a house in the middle of the night to encounter two girls, who appear to be interested in us. We are just going to 'hang-out' and we're doing this why?" "Because the parents are upstairs…" Tony got that grin on his face as he hobble peg-legged his way through the back yards of Miller street. "There's a dog in this one so we're gonna hafta go around front quick." I just followed the lead, but all the time was nervous about the whole scenario.

Finally, we approached her house. It was dark, save for the blue flashes betraying the television in the main room. My heart was racing, but I didn't know why. Was it the possibility of meeting the person who could be my future wife, or the risk of getting caught for the first time? Tony did his traditional tap on the window; we ducked down and waited. Nothing. I felt a certain relief. "Thank God, they fell asleep." "No, just wait." Again he tapped on the window. I went around to the front window to get a peek through the sheers filtering the blue light. I saw the images on the television painting their comatose faces. They were asleep; we were saved. Just then the one jumped as if she had been startled. She got up and walked to where Tony and I had stationed ourselves upon arriving at the house. Now, they *were* up; and the one went to open the door, while the other walked into the other room. I went around the other side of the porch, trying to stifle my footsteps on this old hollow wooden deck. It was another hundred-year-old house. She greeted us with a sleepy smile and helter-skelter hair. The other had obviously gone to the bathroom to primp a little and came out like "morning sunshine". They both gave the customary hug, and we entered the lion's den. They were both attractive, even in the middle of the night, although the room was illumined only by the glare of the television. We had made it in; now what? "You guys want a drink?" I had flashbacks to the first night out.

"Sure." Tony replied. We waited while the two went into the other room. I thought I heard sounds coming from the upstairs. I got scared and said: "You hear that?" "What?" "Sounded like something upstairs." "Just relax, you're just nervous," he said with an air of confidence, "The hardest part is over." The girls returned with glasses and…was that vodka? No…water! They had brought a glass of water. Are you kidding me? I looked over at Tony and he took the water as if it were what he had expected. This was great! No bitter beer, no problem. Just then, I heard the noises again, and this time Tony reacted as well. The only difference was, this time, the noises were accompanied by a pair of legs coming down the stairs. We were caught!

2

I was a hopeless romantic. When I think back about how nervous I was around girls, it doesn't make sense. I thought I had a pretty good sense about what they were looking for, and I wasn't out to take advantage of anyone. Some would call me a romantic, the others might consider me the "king of cheesiness", but either way, I found myself using imagination, once again, in order to gain the affections of the ones who entered my life. I can recall dancing with a girl for her first time, on the hood of my car; because we were down at Little Beaver

Creek late at night, and she was afraid of what lay hiding in the tall weeds. I remember wrapping myself up in a box and being delivered to Millersville, where my girlfriend at the time attended college (Anne is still the finest woman I know). I remember a candle light raft dinner on the pond, in Strasburg, and a portrait of Monica on a cake I made. I remember a blind date, who showed me what it was to really "see." I recall going to the extremes to show these girls how much they meant to me, and the distance I was willing to travel just to see them even if only for a few moments. That was love, and I was no stranger to it. I embraced it when it appeared, and yet over the years would learn the pains that can come with such love. This was not the "puppy-love" of midnight encounters on Miller street. This is the ache you feel when you are separated from that one person; the smile you get when you smell the perfume of the beloved somewhere random, or hear a song that was "your song".

There are those we love, however, that do not love us as we wish they would. How many broken hearts are made from a person who believes they have met their "soul-mate" and yet their "soul-mate" loves them as a "best friend?" You are the guy she tells everything …about other guys. But you are never the *one*. The risks the friend might take to enamour the other are often the devices of tragedy. In an effort to secure love, which can never be secured, can never be forced, one can sever even the original innocent love that appeared at one time to be eternal.

3

It was a weekend seven years ago. It seems like yesterday. I swore on that Monday, I would talk to the two boys I had seen that night, to see whether or not I was dreaming. I have had many dreams about what happened that night, and so it would not surprise me in the least bit if it had been a dream. All the dreams I have had seem every bit as real as that night. That night, however, was different. I felt as though the shackles that had bound me for the last six years previously, had been removed, and I had renewed myself. Six years is a long time to harbor such unrest.

I had a friend in high school, of the feminine gender, with whom I was very close. In fact, I recall at one point in time, she said I was her closest friend in the world. What a remark. Could you get any better than that? We went through high school best friends; graduated best friends; and went on to college, best friends. For my whole freshman year in college there was no one I regarded with higher favor than *Dia*. She knew everything about me, and I knew much about her. We had the perfect, platonic relationship. But that wasn't enough. I was not satisfied, and, in retrospect, now realize that I was probably in love at the time and didn't realize it. It took many years to sort through the details of that relationship.

Dia met a boy in college, and they were in love I suppose. I don't remember too much about him, and thinking back, I can't understand why I saw him as such a threat. In any case, I felt as though Dia no longer needed me as her closest friend because of this newfound relationship. I realize I was terribly wrong about this fact, and later on she probably really could have used a friend. In any case, I decided that if she didn't need me, then I would have to need her. I would have to be in a situation in which I needed her support so that she would place her love and concern back on me. This was the biggest mistake of my life. My worst sin to date that I committed. A sin I would be tormented with for the next six years of my life.

I am a firm believer in purgatory as a place of purification before entrance into heaven; and also believe in a place of eternal torment known as Hell. I believe I was in a purgatorial state for those six years.

I would not wish it on anyone. I was satisfactorily happy, don't get me wrong, but there was that constant separation from peace; always that unfinished business that hung over me like a heavy yoke.

I wanted Dia to believe that I would do anything for her. I wanted her to believe that I cared so much that no one would ever hurt her. At the same time, however, I wanted her to help me. I wanted her to be concerned about me and what I was going through in life. For this reason, the lie began. Oh what a tangled web we weave, until we strangle in that web. I began telling lies about what I was doing, and involved in, so that she would become concerned with me. She would worry about me and, therefore, give me the attention that I craved. I gave the impression that I was involved with certain groups of occultist people, and that I was having thoughts of suicide. At the time, this couldn't have been farther from the truth. I was relatively happy, had a stable college career and hobbies on the side, and was a strong Roman Catholic. But what I was, and what I had to have her believe I was, were two different things. She began to call me more, and talk to me more, and was generally concerned. The lie was paying off, with no consequences. That was the mortality of the sin. The lie was paying off for *me*, but for her it was providing worry and anguish over my situation. She was in an internal tug-o-war trying to decide how to help me with my problems, while at the same time, keeping our "closest friendship," confidence. I kept pushing on with the lies until finally she did what any dedicated friend would do. For fear that I might resort to extreme measures, because of this pseudo-depression, she talked to her parents.

I remember the call I made to her house that night after work, and probably will for the rest of my life. She wasn't very talkative, and I knew something was wrong, so I asked what the problem was. She said, "I told my parents." I remember seeing my world crash in around me. I strangled on the silk threads of the web. How the conversation ended

I don't remember because I was in a daze. It would only be a matter of time before my parents found out, and then my life was over… or so I thought.

My parents, like most I can imagine, probably "jump the gun" at times, over-react, and overprotect their children. If attention was what I sought at this point, you better believe I got it. My parents received a call from Dia's parents with respect to this whole episode. They filled my parents in completely. I don't know what was said, and probably never will, but my parents were plenty concerned. My father wanted me to get counseled or placed on medication for depression. My mother didn't know what to think. I felt betrayed, but not by Dia, or her parents, or my own parents. I felt betrayed by myself. What a stupid thing to do. Only in retrospect do we often see such things in their raw form.

Please don't interpret this next statement the wrong way. I personally don't see a use for most psychiatrists other than that of a springboard for those who can't cope with life. Let me explain this statement. People with chemical imbalances, tragedies in their life, those who are going through an illness, or have experienced a trauma definitely need some sort of counseling or medication from individuals who know how the mind works and such. Most people, however, I believe just need someone to listen to them. This should not cost $120 an hour or more. People get depressed. People get lonely. People get angry. People get "stuck". It is called life (as my mother so fondly reminds me from time to time). Many people use drugs, alcohol, or some other vice to elude these problems. Some choose the alternate path. That is what I did.

Growing up, I knew many people who would go see a psychiatrist and be placed on medicine that either didn't work, or had such extreme side effects that it required subsequent medications to counteract the side effects of the first. I knew kids who were basically given "feel good" pills for when they had lows. I cannot be convinced that there are not more natural ways to handle these situations; however, I suppose those ways were deemed the easiest. I was determined that: 1) I would not see a shrink, and 2) I would not take any medications. What I *would* do is GROW UP! And that is what I did.

4

My life changed about February of that year, when a good friend, Stephanie, called and asked if I would walk her over to the Campus Health Center. You'll read about it in the chapter *Transformation*. I decided that I had two choices. I could either continue to feel sorry for myself for the stupidity I showed in losing a friend, or I could try to live my life the best I could. I decided that I would move on, not forgetting what had happened, but learning from it. I learned some very important precepts that I have kept with me and passed on to others.

The first is: don't take friends for granted. You can never have too many, and the ones you have are invaluable. The second is: smile and the world smiles back. This one is true in ninety-nine percent of the cases. The third is: know that you are a very talented, handsome, intelligent, imaginative, being of which there is no other. So show these talents and attributes whenever possible. Be confident, and others will see confidence in you. The last is: don't be afraid to love. The most powerful gift we have is love.

5

Since those days I have lived out these precepts to the best of my abilities, and have been very happy because of them. My silver cloud had always had a gray lining, however, because of what I had done to a wonderful friendship. Since then I had many dreams in which Dia is hugging me, or holding my hand; we are going out somewhere together, or she is talking with me about what happened. I have had dreams so real that I woke up with tears in my eyes, because I was so happy that we had made up and were friends again. I had prayed. I had prayed that some day we would be reconciled.

I called her house about four years after our bond had been broken, and spoke briefly to her father. I apologized for what I had done, and he suggested that I seek some counseling. He was not being dismissive or defensive but he was sincerely concerned for me. I called because I had my life together, and Dia was the only missing link; the only thing I had never resolved, and the yoke was becoming heavier.

The year after calling, I had secured a position at a Catholic school as a science teacher, and had many students, both young and old, that were intent on going to the Catholic High School in the area and some that already attended the school. Having been an alumnus who had roles in all of the plays and musicals, I was given a pair of tickets to the spring musical that year. I walked into the auditorium, and as I did my heart began to pound, and I began to sweat all over. Dia was there. I guess I should have suspected that she might be, and perhaps in my heart, I knew, but nothing could prepare me for that night. She was present with her husband, her two parents and the rest of the family. I was a stone. I couldn't move, nor did I want to. They sat down a few rows in front of us, and we watched the first half of the musical. At the intermission they got up and walked around, not acknowledging that I was even there, but I think they saw me nonetheless. With the end of the musical, the lights came on, and people began to file out. I couldn't find Dia, but her mother was moving back toward my row. She acknowledged my sister with a smile and a hug, and I thought that she would ignore me, but she extended her hand and simply said: "Hi Mike. How are you?" She said it very sincerely; not as most people do, in passing. I just smiled and replied: "I'm doing really well, thank you." She will never know how sincere my "thank you" really was. That was all, and the dreams continued. I prayed.

6

Tonight was the spring musical at my Catholic High School. A year later my former eighth graders, now freshmen, had some parts to play this year so it was an extra treat. I went to the show anticipating a real treat; little did I know… I got to the school early and spoke to all of my "kids" waiting in line to get in, and just hanging out until time for the show. Finally I was seated with the nice family that bought my ticket for me this year, and was conversing with the couple next to me. I wanted to use the restroom before the play, not knowing when I would get another chance, and so I excused myself and strolled down to the lavatory. It is amazing the memories that flood the mind with certain odors; and that of the lavatory is an odor that remains on file in my olfactory "data base".

I was on my way back to the auditorium when I saw two of my eighth graders kicking a ball around outside and jokingly yelled, "What're you kids doin' out here!" I turned around to head back in and was only a few inches away from a pair of green eyes. The words were simple, but the time seemed like hours that I silently looked at her and she at me. My body froze, and my heart was pounding. "Hi Michael. How have you been?" The words were bound in my throat. All of the time I had spent on car rides, in the shower, in bed at night, thinking about what I would say to her if given the chance, was for naught. Before I could think, she moved closer and embraced me… she held me for a while. My two students *Murph* and *Crocuta,* were standing nearby, but I don't know what they were doing, or whether they even saw this. I put my arms around her and held on like there was no tomorrow. Six years was a long time.

I finally found some words in my throat that were not caught, and said: "I'm good." We let go, and then she said, "I know you called about two years ago, but I just got the message tonight." And she followed up with a smile and a giggle. This set me at ease, and I did what comes natural and said: "Maybe you need to get an answering machine." With that she laughed. The boys were still standing there, and I wanted some privacy with her. I had so much to say, and no time to say it. I began walking down the hall with her, and we were catching up slightly. At the end of the hall, I saw her father. She introduced me to her husband, and then I shook hands with her father. We said our good-byes, and went in to see the show. I don't remember the show.

In all my dreams I had never dreamt it would turn out this way. It is still so surreal to me that I have finally been reconciled. The yoke has been lifted, the gray lining is gone, and now I begin anew once again. I almost feared death that night, because it appeared that the last loose thread in my life had been mended once again. The love that was not, at least was vindicated in some sense. And although I would never completely recover that loss, I would learn to love better because of it.

7

Those legs coming down the stairs at Heather's house were now accompanied by a face. "What....what is this!? What are you boys doing in here." Man, we were so busted! "You get outa here before I call the police." Well, that's all we needed to hear. I froze, unable to move. What now? There I was, speechless. Tony grabbed my arm and we were flying out the door as I looked at Heather and squawked, "I'll see you". I was trying to salvage the evening and trying to be polite, but it was too late for that. "Some first impression that was." We finally paused for only a minute. "Man you can haul butt with that immobilizer on!" He responded as he had so many times before: "I didn't win the cross-country race for nothin'." And although that race was in elementary school, he used that quote when he had the need for speed. We finally made it to Jackson street. If we turned right we would go to the pool; if we turned left, it was the way to the caves. We regrouped and decided to go back to our own houses. "If she calls the cops," he said, "it's better that we're at our own houses." "Fair enough". We departed and went back home.

I didn't sleep a wink. Part of it was adrenaline while the other part was worry. Is this what the whole "girl thing" was going to be like? If so, I didn't want any part of it. You can have it. But then I smiled…talking to myself as I often did. "It was great though, wasn't it? They were pretty weren't they? And interested in us?" I just laughed. It wouldn't be the first time I laughed over a girl, and there would be times when tears were more prevalent than laughter. But I wouldn't have changed a thing, you know. Because each scar, although it changes the skin forever, certainly makes it tougher, and interesting…and provides a great story.

This picture was taken in the early days, by Tony's mother, sitting in her chair. We are preparing to head down to Little Beaver Creek for some fishing.

Tony and I heading out the door at my house. More than likely heading up to see "Sam" at Pizza City.

This was break time for Tony up at the pool. An opportunity for me to try hitting him with the ball as he sailed off the board.

We were getting ready to head out to the beach for the weekend with his youth group...obviously in the eighties.

This was the evening of his bachelor party. The sleeping arrangements were standard, although every now and then, he would use the chair.

This picture was pretty standard as we were driving to our next destination. It's kind of blurry because he never slowed down enough to get it right.

Classic picture from Tony's wedding. "Give us a kiss before they get here."

This is a picture of Tony and his parents, George and Joyce Strubel. Beside Tony is his sister Teri and his brother Ted.

Tony and his wife Mis, with his two children, Tyler and Brooke.

Picture from 1981. My Mom and Dad; Joe is next to Mom, and I'm
the other one. Then from left to right: Theresa, Beth, and Elaine.

This was the sugar cube castle I made for a girl one time. When I look back on some of the things I did to impress my significant others, it floors me.

CHAPTER THIRTEEN

Fire

1

After talking with the lady who had brought the trashcans to the curb, we were ready to begin this game of fooseball. The conversation was painting images and producing sounds we had long abandoned in the recesses of our minds. We began to kick the ball from curb to curb as was the customary warm-up, but now the games would begin, and the conversation would continue. We made our way to the corner... the first one. Tony crossed and stood in the grass at the corner facing mine. I could kick from the corner and get double points or I could stand on the person's lawn and get triple. I always tried for the triple if I felt lucky. I placed the ball in the dew laden grass; I eyed up the target and kicked. As I did, I lost my cigar, and it hit the grass with a slow sizzle. The ball careened off a recycling bin and into the grass; no points. I asked for the lighter so I could re-ignite the cigar that had been dimming for some time. I really don't even know why we smoked the things. We hated the smell, and we just kept spitting to get the taste out of our mouths...but it was a part of the experience. As I lit the cigar, Tony quipped: "You want a blowtorch? How about we try lighting it in my garage." A smile crept across my face, as I relived a moment: the odors, the heat, and the fear.

2

Based on all of our adventures together concerning fire, one might draw the conclusion that we were pyromaniacs. We were not, however, pyromaniacs; we were kids. It is probably one of those stages psychologists speak of all of the time like the "selfish stage," or the "oral stage." We went through our "playing with fire stage." What they say about this stage, we found to be true: "If you play with fire, you're bound to get burned."

Any experiments with fire down at the caves were out of the question. At least for now. Our little run-in with the amishman made an impression that was bound to last at least through early adulthood; however, maybe that's a stage as well. We had to find another place to do our experiments. Logistically speaking, it was next to impossible for us to do anything down at my house. Although my parents both worked, with one brother and three sisters around, nothing remained a secret...nothing. If we learned nothing else from the sledding incident, (see chapter on 'sledding') it was that when you have that many people who know about something, one, if not more, is bound to tell. Tony had an older brother and sister. His sister had been married and lived in Indiana. She wouldn't be a problem, and Ted, his older brother, was at college, so he was also out of the picture. Tony's parents both worked as well. After looking at this big picture, the decision was made. We would experiment at his house.

We realized that to do this experiment outside would be stupid. His house was surrounded by neighbors, most of whom had contact with his parents. We decided, ironically enough, that the safest place to do our blow torch experiments was in his garage. Now Tony lived in an old nineteenth century house, so the garage was detached, and looked like a small square stone barn. It was large enough to fit a car into, and wide enough to fit all kinds of other vehicles like bikes and tractors in as well. No car was in the garage this day, and so the experiments began.

I think it is important to stress at this time that the things we did, we did not knowing what the consequences could have been, nor did we know about the nature of fire and the fuels we were using. Had we known, we never would have even touched the stuff. You hear about children every year who die in fires after playing with matches, lighters, etc. I know that we were blessed by some unseen guardian angels, because we should not have survived most of the stuff we did.

Tony and I went into the garage with a new Spray 'n' Wash bottle that was about half filled with fuel. We had an old book of matches we secured from the local mini market. They usually kept them in a little box on the counter so that when people bought cigarettes, they could take a book with them. We were both thinking about what happened the last time with the amishman, and we were a little shaky. I lit the match and heard it hiss as a blue flame turned yellow and danced on the end of the taper. Tony held the bottle in his right hand, aimed at a spot on the stone floor of the garage, and pulled the trigger. Nothing happened! Based on previous experience, we realized that the nozzle was still in the *off* position. We both looked up and smiled at each other, probably because we realized that it was out of nervousness that we had forgotten to unlock the nozzle. He turned the end of the nozzle clockwise until it read "stream." My match had long since gone out. I struck another. Nothing happened. I struck this match until it bent beyond repair, and pulled another. I was taking no chances with this one, because remember, matches were a scarce commodity. I placed the tip of this match between my thumb and the rough-striking strip

107

on the book and quickly pulled out the match. It lit with a snap, and hissed its disapproval.

I held the match at arm's length and shielded my eyes as Tony gently squeezed the trigger. With a roar of light, the shower of flame leapt forward. I could feel the heat against my skin, and recoiled slightly from the grasp of the flame. The match was extinguished, and the stink of spent fuel filled the air around us. Again, I snapped a match to life, and as I did another rush of fuel was engulfed by the thirsty flame. After a brief roar, the flame disappeared as suddenly as it had surfaced. We stood staring at each other, as if waiting for some revelation. Finally an idea came along.

3

"Ouch!" "I told you Tone, you shouldn't have shot the lady with the baby." I don't know what we were thinking. I remember very vividly painting the room when I got back from college. I decided with all we did in that room the least I could do is patch the holes for my parents and paint the room again. Tony and I had pretty much butchered the room. On this particular day, it was raining outside. Our imaginations were wild, as you've probably noticed by this chapter. I had to make a model of the Roman Colloseum for history class at Lancaster Catholic. I was an artistic type, so I really entered into the project. By the time I was finished, I had a Roman colloseum made from sugar cubes. I took clay and made the gladiators, the fans, and the city folk who walked around it. One of these simple characters was a woman with a baby.

On this rainy day, Tony and I had nothing to do. Two fourteen year-olds with nothing to do…well that spells trouble. All we had was a b-b gun, a carton of bb's and a sugar cube colloseum with little clay targets. What more do you want. We began to shoot at the colloseum and the bb's shattered the cubes. Some of the levels were five sugar cubes thick. But what was most fun, and challenging was shooting the little, inch high clay figures. The game began. What we noticed, however, was that sometimes the bb's richocheted and came back at us. We decided for safety to get behind the folding closet doors (at least we were thinking safety…right?). Tony took aim and said he was going to shoot the lady with the baby. I warned against it: "Don't mess with a mama and her baby." "Quiet and let me concentrate." He just laughed and raised the Red Rider bb gun into position like a sniper through a window pane. He was peeking through the crack in the folding closet doors. He pulled the trigger and we heard a pop with two clicks which followed, "Ouch!" He had indeed shot the woman, and somehow, her hand shot through the crack in the closet door and struck his face. Now, we were scared. Tony gave the gun to me. He was finished. "That was just too weird," he said. "I told you. Don't mess with them mammas."

4

Tony sprayed a spot of fuel onto the concrete floor of the garage. I lit a match and tossed it effortlessly onto the spot of fuel. Nothing happened. I began to experience deja-vous from the cave experience and spraying the soil with fuel when we were there. Tony sprayed twice as much this time, and a small puddle began to form. I snapped off another match, and tossed it into the puddle. It went out on the way down. I squatted down, as if examining a rare find in an archeological dig, and focused my attention on the puddle, as I carefully struck another match. The fuel was beginning to evaporate, so I had to be quick and the match had to strike true. The match reluctantly sighed with a new yellow flame. The smell of Sulfur filled the air as the flame came to life. I held the match about two inches away from the outer edge of the puddle, and dropped it. The sound that the igniting fuel made will remain in my mind forever. It sounded like a parachute catching in the wind, or a flag snapping in a strong gust. The puddle ignited explosively, in a flash of light and sound, and then disappeared as suddenly as it had appeared. Wow! What power. We had this wonderful explosion that lasted less than a second, but was brilliant in color and sound. How could we make it last longer? The answer was simple: supply more fuel.

We decided that we would continue to spray fuel on, once the puddle was ignited. If we continued to supply the fire, surely it would drink more and more of the fuel, and thus sustain its brilliance. Tony made the initial puddle with the fuel again and, as before, I struck the match and held it just inches away from the edge of the puddle. I dropped the match and the monster roared to life. As the beast roared, Tony fed it fuel, and it would roar again, as if showing its approval of our gift, and so the feeding continued. As Tony continued to feed the flame, it began to grow and spread. Remember there was a slight difference between soil and cement. Soil was absorbent and sucked down most of the fuel we sprayed. This new substrate, however, provided a watertight surface, for which it was made. The fuel began to accumulate on top of the smooth garage cement. As it did, the fire's diameter grew wider, and its height approached about a foot. Tony noticed that each time he sprayed, it was as though the fiery beast was roaring. To make a larger roar, he would bring the bottle closer, for more force. Our adrenaline was pumping now, and we wanted more. This little bit was not nearly enough. Each time the bottle inched closer to the mouth of the beast Heraclitus would have called the *Logos or god*. (Heraclitis: Philosopher who examined "change" in the universe, called flux. He described change as unity in diversity and therefore there must be something which changes , and he argued that this something was "fire".)

Time was speeding by so quickly, and we were advancing in our activities to the point where all good senses were lost. We were drugged by this power over the fire or its power over us, so Tony began to become careless. In his last attempt to get a large roar from our now sizable pool or fire, he held the bottle dangerously close. The two of us were past the point of pondering consequences. We were seduced by a power, we really had no control over, into a dangerous trap. Tony held the bottle and sprayed the creature to life. As it roared to life, its sharp claws of scarlet shot out and lunged at that source of its energy and life. Tony's hands felt the burn of the fire and dropped the bottle…. the bottle was plastic. As it dropped into the pool of fuel the flames began to melt the plastic, and with this thin container no longer complete, the fuel leaked out, engorging the beast to dangerously large proportions. For the first time, we felt a different emotion. Not one of elated wonder or power; but, for the first time that day, we felt fear. Now the consequences became clear and reality set in. There was no one to get us out of this… it would be all up to us.

5

Cradling my badly broken wrist, I was now in fourth gear, and the heat was climbing up my arm like a fire on a fuel trail. I was approaching the pool where Tony was working, but had forgotten that the road was a one way street, and I would be going the wrong way. I got close enough to see a red-white blur and knew it was that "Do Not Enter" sign, typical of those streets. The pool was literally a hundred yards away. I turned to the right and heard the engine groan as I ground the gears into second. I rounded the corner and headed toward home. I was starting to feel faint. I had never fainted in my life, but now I was coming to know what it felt like. The sweat was pouring off of me, despite the air conditioning at hurricane strength, and each time I looked at my broken hand, it grew in size and tint. I don't remember much after this, but I was relieved the moment I pulled into the drive of my house. I sat in the driver's seat…I can't remember how long. I just could not move.

6

How many fire safety courses had we been through already?! A flood of memories came to us regarding what to do in case of a fire. Most of them were either, "Get out of the house and call the fire department." or "Stop. Drop. And roll." These did not help in this situation, and there was no way we were calling the fire department. There was smoke beginning to come out of the garage, and we knew there were neighbors out and about, so we pulled the door almost completely shut. There was an old cotton blanket folded against the tractor on the left side of the garage with an array of other garden tools and machines. It smelled of dust and mold. We decided to smother the fire with this dry-rotted blanket. Please forgive our stupidity… we were only kids. I realize now, as a chemist, that cotton is very absorbent and flammable after being in a dusty garage for a few years.

In any case, we took the remnant, unfolded it and laid it down like a picnic blanket on the fire very quickly, and then, (please hold your disbelief, and remember we were kids) quickly lifted it up again, as though we were giving smoke signals. The beast roared to life as though it were now, not only bigger, but bigger and really ticked off. Again fear held us tightly in its grasp, and we searched for another plan. What do fire fighters use under certain circumstances? Water. Which is more dense, water or fuel? Which will float on the other? You will never guess.

I ran around the back of the garage to look for a spigot, and found none. So I continued on around the garage to the right side, and still there was no spigot. I looked up the driveway toward the house, and there it was. The spigot was there, and the hose wound. I ran up and grabbed the hose and began to unwind it. Tony was suffering from smoke inhalation, while coming out of the garage at intervals to catch his breath. He was keeping watch over the fire, and trying to keep it within a boundary, as the fuel was continuing to drizzle out of the melting container. The smell was awful, and there was black smoke wafting out of the garage. I pulled the hose until it reached about five or six feet past the edge of the house… that was it! We were out of hose. We had about fifteen feet to go to reach the fire, and it was growing rapidly. Beside the garage sat an old watering can, in an overgrowth of weeds. It was our only chance. We would have to fill the watering can, and dump it on the fire. We did just that. We filled the watering can and then, comically enough, sprinkled the water on the fire. The monster snapped a growl of disapproval, and began to move? The fire was actually moving, like a snail, or slug, slowing gliding over the surface of the garage. Only later, in retrospect, did we realize that fuel floats on water, and thus the fire would remain untouched. The sprinkling did reduce the intensity a little, but the fire was now spreading in diameter. We had to think quickly, because this *water thing* was just not working.

Tony's eye caught the corner of the garage, and by the time he made eye contact with me, I was already heading in the direction of his previous gaze. I grabbed the shovel and went out back to the side of the garage, and began to dig up the loose soil. I brought in a scoop, and held it over the fire. This was our last act of defiance. We were not going to be beaten. I was scared, not knowing what would happen, but sprinkled the soil down onto the blaze. As I did the fire let out a hiss of disapproval, as if it were, oddly enough, burning…or burning out. I ran and got another scoop, and this time placed it directly on the fire. The fire now was gasping for air as I placed the smothering soil on top of the monster, covering it with a brown blanket. Not only was the soil smothering the fire, but it was also absorbing the fuel/water mixture. How simple a concept; unless you don't know the concept. We should have figured we could absorb the fuel the same way it was absorbed at the caves. The fire subsided with a last gasp of breath, which emanated from the blanket of soil, like a thin ghostly ribbon. The beast was dead.

We both hunched down, and looked at each other. We had greasy brown smudges on our faces, and hands; our shoes were soaking wet, and we were beat. Our eyes then widened, as we thought, almost simultaneously: who saw us?! There had to have been witnesses. We slowly slid back the door of the garage, letting in the sweet outside air, and letting out the poison plastic smell that had filled every space in that garage. I never thought fresh air felt so nice, as I did that day. We surreptitiously looked about to make sure no one was "nosing around" and then began cleanup. We shoveled up the tainted soil and put it into the spot where we got it, in order not to make a visible hole where none had been before. We used the broom to sweep up the remaining soil, and then had a meeting of the minds. We were afraid that when Tony's parents drove into the garage, the car might blow up. Again, we didn't know much about the nature of fuel, and so we tried to come up with some way to test the field before we had to find out the hard way. We were looking for something similar enough to a car that it would be practical for an experiment, but non-expensive enough that it wouldn't matter if it blew up. We decided on the push mower. Tony started it up with a rip of the cord, and ran it over the space a few times. Nothing happened that would indicate danger, but for good measure, we used the weed-eater as well.

Sometimes it is necessary to reinvent the wheel, in order to understand completely something in our lives. We can't always take the word of others as the gospel truth. We learned an important lesson that day. We would no longer take fire and its mysterious nature for granted. Nor could we take for granted Divine Providence. We knew we were under the gaze of Another greater than we, and that we had others to thank for our lives, and fortune that day.

CHAPTER FOURTEEN

The Helicopter: From Paper to Plywood

1

We would not be so lucky in dealing with another kind of *fire*. Now that girls were becoming part of the picture, we were bound to experience fear again. Now we were dealing with something we could not control. These girls had minds of their own and communicated differently than we did. We did like having them around, but it was never without stress. Our lives were limited only by imagination. The more people you invite into your world, however, the more variables there are to deal with. And we were not the exception.

2

Often, when I think back on the times we spent together, it appeared then that we had so much time on our hands everyday. It is only in looking back now, that I realize what little time we had. Everyday to us was an endless opportunity for adventure. In order to accomplish these adventures, we needed certain resources. Because we weren't adults, and didn't have money, we had to do what we could with what we had. This meant improvising. One of our concerns was transportation. Mind you, the bikes were excellent for getting around, especially with the adaptations made to them. However, we needed something that could go farther distances. In the show, *The A-team,* these guys usually had two main modes of transportation. The first was a black van, that was suped up like a hot rod sort of vehicle. The other vehicle was a helicopter. After looking at the options, our minds went to work. Unfortunately, by this time, the recreation program at the local park was over, so we needed to find a new hangout. The local pool worked out nicely. It was much closer than the park, and was a nice place just to relax, if nothing else. We had our meetings in the boys' bathroom. Katrina couldn't be a part of this of course, (although she may have tried) but at any rate, this is where we would draw up our plans, and decide what to do next.

The helicopter was by far one of the most ambitious operations that we ever undertook. We had made up the plans, taking into consideration that it had to be a two-seater, and had to have some kind of defense system. What a helicopter it was too... at least on paper. The design I had drawn in a composition book, has long since been lost. Now don't laugh, but the whole concept being used here was "pedal power." The helicopter had a lower sprocket with pedals that had a chain like a bike. The chain would turn a gear higher up, and the gear would turn a smaller gear that was horizontal, which would subsequently turn the propeller, and thus we would achieve flight, right? Well, it looked good on paper anyway. We had our final plans, and in my mind, I could see us floating effortlessly through the blue skies with this wooden helicopter. Oh... did I forget to mention... we were to build this helicopter out of WOOD! It doesn't get much better than that. As it turned out, that day was less about building a helicopter and more about strengthening old friendships. We didn't have money, or resources, so we had to improvise. We gathered all the building supplies we could find. We got everything from bean poles (propeller) to plywood, and two-by-fours. We were set to go. How would we put this together? Nails, of course.

We started up one summer morning. We met up at Tony's place, behind his garage, and got together all of the necessary tools and supplies. The work began. We started by laying down a foundation of the wood, based on the primitive plans. We laid down what each side of the "chopper" would look like, and then began to build the main platform, to which the skis would be attached. The two skis consisted of baseboard molding placed with the inside down, with two-by-fours attached, one at each end of the ski, so that they created a flat ski, with two foot-long boards sticking up about a yard apart. The skis themselves were only about five feet long. Keep in mind that we didn't have any electric tools, so any sawing we had to do, was done by hand. For this reason, we kept sawing to a minimum. Sometimes, things were a little crooked, or rough, but we found it easier to overlook small discrepancies rather than have to saw more wood. We had worked now for about an hour, and were pleased with the amount of work we had done. That would turn out to be the only solid hour we worked that entire day. In fact, we didn't get much more done on the helicopter that day. The reason for this delay? One word… Katrina.

3

After our first hour of work, Katrina (Amy) came along. She lived only a short distance down the block, so it was nothing for her just to walk down. She asked what we were doing, and we consequently told her. She wanted to help, but we had a plan, and knew what we had to do. So we rejected her generous offer, in the best interests of the "team." As it turned out, maybe it would have been in our best interests to let her help after all. She left in a bit of a "huff", and we did feel a little bad that she couldn't help, but we soon forgot why we had stopped working in the first place, and resumed our sawing and hammering. About fifteen minutes passed and Katrina returned. She had with her a tray of cookies, and juice of some sort. "Time to take a break," she said. "You guys have been working hard, so it is time for you to take a snack break." What could we do? She was here with her tray; we wouldn't let her help build, so she found some other way to help the team. We decided we would stop and take a break. We were kind of hungry, and it was beginning to get hot again, so the juice would hit the spot. As we were eating and drinking, Katrina walked over and circumspected the operation. She was perusing the mess with a critical eye, but she didn't ask any questions. Tony just looked in my direction and rolled his eyes as though he was saying: "Just let her look, and then she'll leave us to our work." We finished up the cookies and drinks, and thanked Katrina for her concern, and then once again we began to work.

As Katrina cleaned up the cups, etc. and began to leave, she mentioned that she would be willing to do whatever she could to help us. We told her for the second time that this was something we had to do on our own. She left once again, in less than a happy mood. At this point, Tony and I were putting on the platform. We had a piece of plywood that was about three feet long and three feet wide. This would be the main platform from which all other pieces would attach. Once the two skis were attached to the plyboard, we stood it up on the skis to test the support. The plywood wobbled as we touched it, to the left and right. We knew from this test, that it would never support us, so we put two-by-four supports between the two ski supports. This helped to support it better, but it still wobbled quite a bit. As we were trying to determine where our engineering had gone wrong, Katrina once again approached us. This time, she had no food, but began to ask questions, in an attempt to draw us away from the project at hand. "Tony, do you and Mike want to come over and play 'Ghost,' or 'Haunted House'?" Usually we would jump at the chance, because they were fun games, and she knew that her offer would be enticing, but Tony looked at me, and I at him, and in unison, we replied "No. We are in the middle of an important project. We don't have time for playing around today," Tony replied. Katrina said, "FINE!" and stomped off in the direction of her house once again.

About half an hour passed, and we were beginning to get the main foundation to become stable, when Katrina approached a third time. This time she had soda and sandwiches. "You guys must be hungry. Why don't you take a break and have some lunch." "Lunch!" Tony said. "It's only ten-thirty!" "You guys have been working hard though, you must want something to eat. Come on and take a little break." What could we do. She made sandwiches and went to all of this trouble. (Looking back now, I can see what a cry for attention this was. We must have been terrible. She just wanted to play with us.) Tony looked at me, and I at him, and reluctantly said, "Okay. We'll take a break. But when we finish eating, we can't take any more breaks. We need to get this done today." Now we didn't have any of the other things we needed like seats, sprockets, etc. but we also weren't really looking towards the end of the project as much as we were at simply getting the thing built. We ate the sandwiches, and they were tasty, and then thanked Katrina once again and bade her farewell. She left, not so much with a "huff" this time, as with a mischievous smile. She knew something, and it bothered us to no end, that we were the subject somehow, of her entertainment.

We resumed our work yet again. We were running out of nails, so we began to ration them. We were using finishing nails and ten-penny nails, which are huge. We must have given the impression that we were building a house, with all the noise that was coming from the back yard. We were really beginning to sweat, but that was good, because it meant that we were working hard. It was approaching about twelve o'clock. We had finished most of the foundation and were ready to begin attaching the sides, when Katrina entered from the front yard. "When are you guys gonna be finished with this thing? Is it really gonna be able to fly?" We ignored her, and decided that if we were ever going to finish, we would have to continue to ignore her. She proceeded to ask more questions, to which we simply answered, "I don't know," or "What's it to ya?" Needless to say, we were pretty irritated at this point. She stomped off in that style that was so familiar to us, and for which we held her most dear.

We were about to attach the sides that we had put together, when Katrina reappeared just at the edge of the yard. Not fifteen minutes had passed, and she was walking very slowly in our direction. "What is it now Katrina?" Tony said. "I think there's something in my house," she said. "What do you mean?" Tony asked. "I am hearing things upstairs. Maybe it's the ghost up there." Now Tony and I were always looking for a new adventure (if you haven't figured that out yet), and I do believe this was the secret smile that Katrina had. She knew that we could never resist an invitation into the unknown. "Are you sure?" I said, with a skeptical tone to my voice. "Yes. I heard the noises coming from upstairs." I asked, "What did the noises sound like?" This is why I was the brain in the bunch. I knew that although Katrina was crafty, she would not have thought ahead to further questioning on the noises. She looked at me like a spoiled child who does not get the candy in the supermarket. The child who is deliberating whether or not they should simply accept defeat, or cry in an attempt to win the war. I think Tony saw this "look," and to spare her the embarrassment of catching her in an elementary lie, he said, "Let's go check it out." If Tony said there was a sound that needed checking, then there was no doubt in my mind. I knew what he was thinking, and I knew of his devotion to Katrina. We were going to check it out.

We got to Katrina's house, and the first words out of her mouth were, "Do you guys wanna play something?" She was busted. She didn't say anything about the sound she had heard, about being afraid, or anything of the sort. It wasn't until Tony said, "Did it come from upstairs?" that she finally snapped back and remembered the reason why we were here. We went upstairs, and there was no sound. We searched the house, and heard and saw nothing. We gave it our best investigation, and she seemed satisfied. But when we turned to leave, she thought she heard the sound again. We stayed for about five minutes to listen for the sound, and nothing happened. Finally, we told her that we really needed to finish this project, and not to bother us any more. She turned from us, sulking, and we left.

We arrived back at our, yet to be made, helicopter, and once again began to put on the sides. As it would turn out, the sides would never get attached to the helicopter. As we were placing them on, Katrina made an appearance once again. Although I don't know what it was for this time, whether snacks, spooks, or an inquisition, it didn't really matter. We would never get the helicopter finished. She must have returned five or six more times that day, with many different schemes with which to distract our attention.

Although I seemed very annoyed at the time (and I was), I can't help now but to look back with a great love for Katrina. She really had a deep devotion to the two of us, and I know we would have done anything for her… we still would. When I think back on those times, the most favorable memory of that day was not building a helicopter, for it never got built, but the love that a girl had for her two friends, and her need to be loved by them in return. Well, we did love you Katrina. We did then, and do still. It's the old adage: "You can't live with them, and you can't live without them."

4

Tony attempted to get the three-point bonus by kicking the ball from the person's lawn onto the curb. He paused. There was a hesitation there, but not because of the shot. The "game" seemed to be the furthest thing from his mind. Then he looked up, took a breath and posed a good question...a valid question: "How *can* you live without them? How are you gonna be without a wife and kids?" I wondered how long he had been waiting to ask that question. How long had it taken him to word it right in his head?

He kicked the ball over and before I saw it, I knew he had doubled his point value, by the gloating, "That's what I'm talkin' 'bout." I thought about his question, which was a common one. "How was it that someone who loved so much, and had dated throughout most of his adolescent and college years could give it all up?" It's a real question, because when we choose one thing, we necessarily reject another. "I don't think of giving something up, so much as I think of what I will receive in return." "What do you mean? You think you're gonna get a better place in heaven because you're doing this?" Tony questioned. "No my Methodist friend", I quipped (this Methodist/Catholic banter went on sometimes for hours. It was all done with due respect and affection of course.) "What I'm saying is that sex is not everything. And the fact that I surrender one thing, does not mean I don't receive other gifts which are more valuable. For instance, I can be truly intimate with thousands of people in a way I could not be if I were married. Can you imagine if I had a wife, and I told her how many different women I was giving spiritual direction to? Can you imagine if I had children, what it would be like when I would tell them again and again, that I have to leave *their* activities in order to attend others with children who are not my own? Not to mention that Christ was celibate and I am called to be the 'other Christ'?" "Well...good for you...not for me." I kicked the ball at him, and it dropped down to hit the corner of the curb and gave me one point. He argued the point, because it hit *him* first, but I knew it counted. I began to think of the friendships I had throughout my life. A smile formed on my face. But what cost does friendship demand? What cost indeed.

CHAPTER FIFTEEN

Sledding

1

I sat in the car while the acidic effervescence was rising to my mouth. Sweat was saturating my clothes and little beads had formed on my arms and legs. My skin was cold and clammy to the touch and I was in a fog. I got out of the car and stumbled into the house. The green and gray was not "road and bank" now, but sidewalk and lawn. I stumbled through that front door which stuck as it had so many times in the middle of the night when we were trying to open it soundlessly. At this point, the sound it made was the least of my concerns, I needed to get inside! I leaned against the door, the last bit of strength left in me was trickling out in the beads of sweat now coating my arms and legs. With one last effort I pushed my weight against the door as if I were pushing through one of the turnstiles in a New York hotel. The door gave under the weight and I stumbled into the kitchen where the lifeless vacuum cleaner lay sprawled across the floor, and that was it! I was slurring my words and remember saying: "I think I broke my wrist" and then collapsed in the floor.

I made it. I had driven home without hitting anything or anyone and now I was safe. Now I could get the help I needed. My mother and little sister walked in and the first thing my mother said was: "Would you get up! Stop fooling around, you're always carrying on." I began to laugh once again. Well, that only incensed her further. "Come on now, are you kidding?" My sister shouted: "Look at his arm." And then there was immediate comprehension. My mother was speechless. She picked up the phone, and I thought: "Good, she's calling the hospital." I heard someone pick up, and she told them that I would not be in to work today. Are you kidding me? She called my work first to tell them that I would not be in. Forget the doctor, or the hospital…she called my employer. Maybe I wasn't safe. Before I knew it we were on the way to the hospital. And then the inevitable question. "What were you doing?" This was going to take some explaining. Was this the stupidest most dangerous thing I'd ever done? I mean aside from the blowtorch thing? No. Nope, not even close. There was that winter.

2

The year was 1986, and it seemed as though, that winter, we had blizzard after blizzard. The streets were white and the drifts of snow that built up at times, were as high as the rooftops. We were obviously out of school because of the horrific weather, and therefore, we were unattended at home. We were certainly old enough to care for ourselves, but with so much snow, there had to be something mischievous we could get into. Earlier that week, we had sneaked out of the house yet again, with another friend of Tony's, Goose. As we made our way through my bedroom window, as tradition, we had decided that since the snow was so deep, we could jump from the pinnacle of the roof into the drift, as opposed to just jumping from the edge of the roof. That is what we did. What a rush for a youngster, but that is another story.

On this not so special day, we decided that it would be just as much fun to jump off the roof, yet again, during the day. This created some problems, however, because my brother was also home from school. Tony came down to the house, and we began to conspire a plan that would allow us to jump off the roof, while at the same time giving us immunity to any consequences. We decided that my brother, Joe, could not *tell on us*, if he was doing the same thing, so we invited him to join us… and join us he did. We began by leaping off of the porch roof into a pile of snow that was partially due to the immense drifts, and partially made by our using a snow shovel to pile it up higher. That was enjoyable for a while, but like so many rushes in life, they soon become commonplace, so we "upped the ante," so to speak. We began jumping from the pinnacle of the roof into another drift on the side of the house. As I leapt from the point of the roof, all I heard was the clean crack of the shingles under my oversized "moon boots" and the swift rush of air past my ears. I was flying. For a few seconds that seemed like years, I was in suspended animation; I was the only one on the planet. Flying forever and then the soft crunch of the snow as I landed knee deep into the drift below. The ride was over and oh what a blast! We began to jump down and land on our sides, our backs, you name it, and we landed on it.

We knew it was too good to last. We knew that at some point my sisters would begin to nose around. As fate would have it, they began to hear footsteps on the roof. We never considered the fact that they might step outside and see us. No sooner had we begun, however, than my sisters arrived on the scene and saw what we were doing, and decided that they too would jump off the roof. Needless to say, this kind of put a wrench in our plans that day. We were sincerely worried about their safety, for a selfish reason. We were not worried for them because we didn't want them to get hurt, however, we were worried for our own lives if something happened to them and it was our fault. If one of my sisters ended up in the ER because we let them do something stupid, we would face the wrath of God... or my father... whichever came first. We allowed my two older sisters Elaine, and Beth to jump off the roof, and into the pile at the base of the porch, but not from the pinnacle. My sisters did not argue about the pinnacle thing, probably because they were scared. Knowing how sisters operate is paramount to being a brother. We could see their fear, and knew what our boundaries were. My youngest sister, Theresa had not yet made an appearance.

After an hour or so of jumping (my sisters quickly tired of this), we all considered what to do next. I don't remember ever being bored as a child, however, the possibility of boredom was an ever-present threat. To be bored is the worst thing a child could be. For this reason, we were not willing to cut our losses and call it a day. We had a palaver on the roof and brainstormed on what our next move should be, while grazing on the crust topped snow covering the roof. The ice had formed a layer on top of the snow, and when we broke through, small sheets of ice glazed with snow came off in our hands. We accordingly ate them like cookies. A plastic toboggan lay in the snow in the back yard before us. There was still a light dusting of snow littering the inside where we had used it previously. The sun was reflecting off of the crystals inside the toboggan like little diamonds. We saw the slope of the roof, and the packed snow on the roof from our path to the pinnacle, and I believe that above each of our heads, I could see a very faint light bulb lit, with the energy emanating from the diamonds. The rest was history.

I don't recall who was first to try this experiment in snow speeding, for it was long ago. Tony would probably claim it was he who took the first slide, and Joe would probably try for the credit as well. I know I wasn't the first to take that fateful ride down the slippery slope, but it really didn't matter, because after the first one went down, we were hooked. "Fffffffffftttt....ppppmmmmffffffff," was the only sound heard and then a cry of triumph and cheers from the rooftop. The sled slid only a few feet off of the roof, with a little improvised ramp at the end. The sled would just drop straight down off the end of the roof into the pile of snow. It was nothing too dramatic, and yet it was a thrill. Then my youngest sister, Theresa, came up to the window and she wanted to try. Now Theresa *was* too young. She cried and whined and that didn't work. She started to climb out the window, and we shut it. Then…the secret weapon; this is the one the sisters always bring to the fore when they find they are unsuccessful in getting what they want. "Let me do it…or I'll tell." "Tell," oh come on. What were we, in elementary school? No, but we weren't stupid either, and she probably would. This could be a bluff. But we acknowledged her bluff and kept the window closed. She tromped off through the room, in a mimic of a miniature Katrina. We went down on our bottoms; on our backs; on our knees; backwards; double; we tried every possible combination that was physically possible, and when we thought we had done it all, Tony came up with the unthinkable. He wanted to go down standing up, as if he were on a present day snowboard. (In fact, I now look back on this episode in my life and swear that someone saw us that day, and came up with the concept for a snowboard.)

Silence chilled the rooftop. No words were exchanged; only looks. He was nuts! Not only was the rooftop slippery, but the toboggan was plastic, and the inside of the toboggan was slippery. Thousands now joined the sparse collection of diamonds that once littered the floor of the toboggan. As Tony stomped his green, lace-front boots into position, more diamonds appeared. I was worried, but said nothing. I think Tony read it in my eyes, but what I saw in his eyes, I would see only three other times in his life. What I saw in its purest, rawest, form was adrenaline. Had I chosen to talk him out of it, I would have failed miserably.

No one said anything. Tony looked back with those crystalline eyes, and a grin formed at the edges of his mouth. "Just a few feet; keep my balance; give a little leap and I'm 'home free'." Then he stepped into the sled, in front of which we had built a small wedge of snow, so that when we sat in the toboggan, it wouldn't slide off without us. He braced his left foot against the front wall of the toboggan, and his right foot against the back wall. He looked first at me, and then at Joe, and then focused his emotionless blue eyes on the white landscape ahead of him. He gently nudged the sled forward and with a low crackling slide, the toboggan began to move forward, and then whoosh! It flew off the roof.

I doubt if even Tony remembers the trip down. I would never forget it. Before my eyes, passed adventures come and gone, birthdays, holidays, and growing up. As our eyes left the white landscape of the yard, and focused on the pile of snow at the base of the roof, a dead calm came over the neighborhood. This thick silence was almost smothering. It probably lasted for a fraction of a second, but that second was the longest I have yet experienced. Tony's body was motionless. As the toboggan left the surface of the roof, it fell to the ground, and with it Tony's support. He dove headfirst into the pile of snow, as a result of the toboggan coming out from under him. He was *pile-driven* into the man-made bank of snow up to his waist, and all that was visible, were his hands and his legs. During that calmness, the pervading thought was: "Has he broken his neck?" After all this time, and all the adventures I couldn't fathom the fact that I would have to tell his parents what had happened. I would have to tell them that a stupid stunt was the cause of their son's injury… or death. I saw their long faces and the anger they had for me in that moment.

3

Tony's parents: George and Joyce, had very little expectations of us. What I mean is that they expected us to be good, and do the best we could, those expectations they made because they would help us and make us better. The expectations I'm speaking of have to do more with personal stuff. They didn't expect us to be quiet at sleep-overs, or keep us from eating dozens of Amish cookies when we were at the house. We were allowed to watch whatever movies were around or we rented, and do just about whatever we wanted in the back yard. I mean we did build a helicopter back there with his dad's wood; and rode a dirt bike; and made a haunted house in his attic.

I'm pretty sure the difference had to do with his siblings. Tony's brother and sister were out of the house, and that left Tony pretty much an only child. We really had free reign. Whenever I would come up, Tony's dad was forever giving me fresh tomatoes and they always had Amish cakes and cookies around. I'd walk in the door without knocking and there would be his mom, knitting and watching QVC while his dad was futzing around outside trying to out-think his arch enemies, the rabbits. They always had a smile, but wouldn't hesitate if we did something stupid. One more than one occasion I heard Tony's dad say, "Awww Michael. Now what were you thinkin'." Those are some of my fondest memories. The last thing I ever wanted to have to do, is report some bad news and cast a shadow over their usually care-free demeanor.

4

I was beginning to plan out my speech to his parents when all of a sudden... movement. His legs started moving like some comical cartoon character that has landed headfirst into a hay bale... or a pile of snow. I gasped, or breathed (I was probably holding my breath) and slowly, Tony got to his feet. His head was caked with snow like an old "Grizzly Adams" movie or Heidi, where the old mountain man-like character has just come out of the blizzard and his beard is frost coated.

Although he was coated with the snow, his dominant fire-orange sock hat was purely visible, and slightly lowered over his brow. He slowly moved his neck and rubbed his head as if he had just bumped it on a closet shelf or a low ceiling. And then… he began to laugh. "Damn!" He said in his half whimpering voice he used sometimes to add a comical seasoning to whatever the situation was. The word was a bit unclear because of the now numb lips that tried to pronounce it. By this time in his life, Tony didn't swear when he was angry, but did it to be funny. There was no disrespect, or bad mouthing, but it was a communication he had with me. Something we both understood that was meaningful. In most cases after he swore he followed it up by saying: "Sorry dear Lord." And then a laugh usually followed. Here, it was comical mostly because his lips were numb and frozen, therefore softening the harshness of such a word with the blatant absurdity of the action that preceded it.

His laugh was the sweetest sound I think I heard that entire day. We all began to laugh then as well, but inside I still wondered, with grave curiosity, how we would have explained a broken neck or anything else to the parents in our lives. I also reflected in an instant how I ever would have survived without that other part of me that was not afraid to do what others would not… could not.

Happy ending?… kind of. My mother arrived home, and true to her threats, my sister Theresa gave her a full debriefing. As good mothers often do, she informed us that we were to, "Just wait 'till your father gets home." When my father did arrive home, he was enraged. He was mad, however, not so much that we were sledding off the roof, but that we did not shovel the driveway as we were told to. I remember him commenting on how we could certainly use the shovels to create a pile of snow, but could not use them for the purpose for which they were intended. Now thirteen years later, I think I understand what he meant… or maybe not. Sledding has never been that good since.

CHAPTER SIXTEEN

Things that Go Bump in the Night

1

We rounded the corner just as the lights were going off in the house stationed right at the intersection of a cul-de-sac and the road on which we were traveling. I had scored another two-pointer to tie the game as the lights dimmed on the house at the end of the street. All we saw was that flashing faint glow that the television makes when one is watching in the dark. This was one of those moments that Tony and I have every now and again when we will see a symbol and recall the same thing. He began to ask me, just as I saw the picture in my head. "Remember that night at Tina's house? It was a tense night." But not as intense as our experience years later at another girl's house. (Do you see a trend here?)

2

As Tony and I got older, we had to get jobs. Don't get me wrong, we've both always worked hard, and now appreciate a dollar. I worked full time at a miniature golf course in Strasburg, where I lived. It was about a mile or two from my house, and the people who owned it taught me a great deal about business and responsibility. Tony worked at the local swimming pool which was about a quarter of a mile from my house, if that. He was kind of a *do all*. He started out teaching swimming lessons, and helping take care of the snack shop, etc. and when he was old enough, later on, became a life guard, which was a job that seemed to have been made just for him. When he got in the pool, he was like a shark as far as swimming. And on the diving board, looking back, he probably could have been a professional diver.

When I wasn't working, I would spend my days at the pool, with Tony, in the summer. There we would plan, and train, and talk about life's questions. That summer was a good summer for me for two reasons. The first is that I got to meet many of Tony's friends, and so began to be associated with that circle, for better or worse. The second reason was that this was the year *Top Gun* came out, which was a popular movie with a lead cast of Tom Cruise. Finally, we had another genre on which to base our lives. We were to be pilots, thus began our new identities.

Top Gun pilots come up with what they call "call signs," or names by which they chose to be acknowledged. Tony's name was *Maverick*, after the star of the movie. My call sign was *Viper Scout*. There were two other guys that we hung out with at the time. The first guy, originally a friend of Tony's, who was older than we were, was called *Goose*, and the second guy was actually in the "A-team" with us. His name was Face back then, but now his call sign was *Jester*. The four of us were together at the pool the one day and ran into a few girls from Tony's school. That was the beginning of the end.

We began talking about possible plans for the evening. This girl told us that her parents were going away for the weekend, and that she had the house to herself. The four of us were invited to spend the night, and she was going to have some friends over as well. Sounded simple right? Well, the problem wasn't sleeping accommodations. I said I was staying with Tony, which in reality I was, and Tony said the same to his parents. We were going to head to the girl's house that night, and stay there. This sounded awfully familiar to me. I was beginning to have flashbacks again to the night we spent with the two girls, and a beer. I felt like I didn't belong. Wouldn't the situation be magnified with more people? The logic I used to convince myself otherwise was this: *If Jester and Goose are there, then I won't be alone. If nothing else, I will be able to talk to them.* That built up my confidence a little bit, but I was still wary and anxious (in the anxiety sense).

It was about ten o'clock in the evening, and Tony and I arrived at the girl's house. It was an old townhouse, and her half of the house was on the left. The two doors were side by side on the front porch. There were lights on in the house, but it was late, and we didn't want the door to be answered by two angry parents, so we were cautious. All we saw were the faint blue flashes from the television. Tony peered through the window, and she was there watching MTV. I knocked lightly on the door, at which time she got up and opened the door with a smile. She had a light jacket on, and looked as though she were heading out.

"My grandparents called, and they are making me stay at their house tonight. Sorry guys. There is stuff in the fridge, and you're welcome to stay as long as you like." Now an interesting dynamic happened at this point. Tony's face dropped, as if his life blood had been drained. Mine, on the other hand, was beaming. We could just go back to Tony's house now and call it a night. A sign from God. Thank you! Could it be this easy? No. The girl left, sincerely sorry (you could see the disappointment all over her face) and Tony and I sat there. "What now?" I asked. I dared not suggest we call it quits. "We wait for Goose and Jester, and see what they want to do," he said.

About fifteen minutes passed, and there was a knock at the door. We immediately jumped. I ran to the back to secure an escape route, and Tony made himself flat against the inside wall. The TV was the only light in the room, so he was hidden by the shadows. Tony then saw a familiar "peeper" looking through the window, and opened the front door. Goose and Jester walked in and planted themselves on the sofa. Now Jester was still just a baby, and he was learning the ways of the world. Goose, on the other hand, *was* the ways of the world, and was ready for a party. "There isn't gonna be any party here tonight. Tina had to go to her grandparents' house." Goose looked at Tony, and Tony looked at me, and I looked at both of them as if saying, "You can't be serious." "We got a house!" Goose exclaimed.

I reported that the back door had no doorknob on it. All that was there was the square crank socket where the knob used to be. I decided it was my personal mission to find an object to fit into that square hole, just in case a back door escape was necessary. The others planted themselves on the couch after commandeering drinks and food from the refrigerator. This was going to be a long night. Because we shared a townhouse, every time someone moved in the other house, or a light went on, we thought we were discovered. There were even a few times when someone walked up on the porch and we thought for sure that the parents had come home early, or we were discovered by the neighbors who called the police. Writing about this evening in daylight isn't so bad, but then, we were there at night, and the adrenaline, mixed with this seeming freedom was like mixing alcohol and medication... each had an adverse effect on the other. I kept having flashbacks of the night we got caught at Heather's house, and thought *that* was the end. Goose and Tony decided that they would take a walk and check out a few things. This left me with Jester.

The two having gone, Jester and I began to chat. It was amazing to me how much he looked up to all of us. Yet in retrospect, I guess if I had three older guys whom I hung out with, I would look up to them as well. He then mentioned to me that he was scared coming here tonight. The fact that he had arrived with Goose, probably didn't help matters any, but he was scared. "I'm not really good around girls. Goose said there would be some here tonight and that I could have my pick. My pick? My pick would've been to leave the girls at home." I let out a belly laugh, but this probably wasn't the best response. Jester already seemed kind of embarrassed about being shy, so I could tell by his response that he was hurt now.

"Listen Jester. I'm about three years older than you are, and I was scared about coming here tonight. And I'm a little more comfortable around girls, but don't appreciate being in that situation at all." I could see he relaxed a little, and yet in his eighth grade wisdom, he appeared to perceive that I was patronizing him, like some adult. So I shared with him the story about my first encounter with the two girls in my neighborhood and how I just wanted to hide somewhere. "When I got here tonight and I heard that the girls weren't going to make it, I couldn't hide the smile on my face. I think Tony saw it, but I didn't care." "Really?" "Yeah. Trust me Jester, that will all come in time, and when it does, it won't be some kinda party you're going to in order to have 'experience'. It'll be this girl you've had your eye on. She'll smile at you and it will make your day. That's all it will take." "Yeah, I have this girl in my class like that. But she hangs out with older guys. She tells me stuff, you know, about her life. But it's not like that." Boy could I relate. That was the time in my life when I was experiencing the "friend phenomenon" with Dia.

"Jester, there is this girl…" BAM! There was a hammer on the back door. BAM! Again it came. I told Jester to monitor the front and I would go out towards the back to see what was up. I scurried into the kitchen, where the back door was, and there was Tony… he was alone. I opened the door with the screwdriver and almost knocked him down, on purpose. "What are you trying to do? You could've tapped. You freaked us out."

2

Tony paused as we reached the corner of the next intersection. This was the part in the walk where there was typically a sprinkler going, so we had to modify our point system, and certainly didn't want to lose the ball in the water. "What do you mean you were going to knock me down! I was the one always getting injured. I was always watching your back. I never hurt you once." "Never?" I said. And then a smile came to his face… "Well…not on purpose." "Well, let's talk about this a little bit.

There was that time we decided to spar at your girlfriend Missy's house, and I was distracted only for a moment, at which point you *clocked* me across the jaw, knocking me across the car. Or maybe I should bring up the time you wanted to see if my air gun could shoot a metal dart through my wallet…while the wallet was still in my back pocket. Perhaps you've forgotten the times we wrestled in the swimming pool, and every now and then I would be getting the upper hand. Right about that time, you would take me under the water and bang my head against the bottom of the pool. You think that is a little extreme?" At this point, Tony had tears rolling down his cheeks… because he was laughing so hard. He had that "tommy-gun Strubel laugh" that was very distinct. Wherever he was, and wherever anyone heard it, they knew he was near.

"But that was little stuff! It was nothing really that serious. I mean we were just foolin' around." And then he started laughing so hard that a sound could not escape. "I know what you're thinking about," I said, as I gave the sprinkler a wide birth, its drops beating the pavement like thousands of fingernails tapping a smooth table. That's what we had told the cop: "We're just fooling around."

3

Ever in training, Tony and I would spar. I would have the nunchakus and he the sais. We were still learning the capabilities of the weapons and our ability to control them. We sparred with these weapons for hours, and were progressing in our aptitude. One night, however, just as the streetlights came on, Tony and I were sparring, when he sliced my side with one of the sais. It was not a deep cut, but just enough to draw blood and get my ire up. I began going at him quickly with the nunchakus, just as the police car was rounding the corner. All Tony said was "cops" and he tossed the sais into the bushes, while I stowed the chucks in the back of my waistband, under my shirt. The cop stuck his head out the door and said, "Where are the sais?" Tony finally obeyed the first law of adolescence: Deny, deny, deny. "What sais?" "What's going on here boys?" the officer smiled. It was a knowing smile. He smiled as if to say *I wish I were your age again.* "We're just foolin' around. Nothing serious, just carrying on." "Do it somewhere else then." "But…this is my yard?" I replied. "Well then do it inside," he yelled. Well, that was that.

4

Tony and Goose had taken a walk down town, but it was a short walk. They had crept around Goose's house, and I think someone was awake who should not have been, so they quickly scurried back to our "safe house." The rest of the night is a bit of a blur. Quite honestly, we were just four guys sitting in someone else's house watching TV. Where was the excitement in that? About three, we decided to go back to our separate houses. Tony and I snuck in by his back porch door and set up in the living room. It was not too long and we feel asleep.

I'm pretty sure it was only a few days later, or maybe weeks, time is kind of blurry now, and Tina approached us again for another overnight. We politely replied that we thought it would be fun, and we'll see about it later, but we had no desire to spend another night there. I was hoping to get to chat with Jester again, about Dia. I felt bad for the kid, and yet even Jester was coming of age. In the days ahead, he would demonstrate a certain level of comfort with girls, even before I would. But always in a respectful way. I can't help but to think that perhaps that night, in a chance meeting of two guys who found each other in a similar situation, that a *koinonia* was shared (Koinonia: Greek word that loosely translates into "mutual understanding, family, intimate connection of ideals). I can't help but to think perhaps what I said in those few minutes we had, might have built the foundation for something to come…perhaps.

CHAPTER SEVENTEEN

Just a Girl...

1

The game commenced, having now rounded the water hole. "Okay, I'll admit I should've been a little more soft with the sai. I should've taken it easier on you. I forgot how tender you are." I stopped kicking the ball. He knew where the buttons were and how to press them. "You wanna go now? I don't want to hurt you. You know, you're old... older than I am." It reminded me of the one time when we *were* going to *go at it*. He laughed it off. "We never really fought over anything though, you know? Most friends would've gotten in many fights by now, I think. But we haven't disagreed on too much." "That's 'cause I'm right!" I replied. "Yeah...right."

2

I remembered that time very vividly. There was one fight...over a girl. The only thing that could seemingly cause a rift between the two of us. She was a girl we both met at the same time. This girl was different, in every sense of the word. Not so much because she was strange, but different in that she was so "up". I can count on one hand the number of girls I have met that are so positive and outgoing. Most, I have experienced are shy at first, regardless of who they meet. This girl was not shy, but was not "easy" in the bad sense of the word either. Some might get the impression that she was only looking for one thing and that explained why she was bubbly and giddy; but honestly, that was just her. She and I very quickly became friends. I had never really been "friends" with a girl like this before. I would only achieve such a level with one other girl in my life...Dia.

At any rate, while I was becoming friends with her, she was becoming a girlfriend to Tony. It was only the natural course of things. Some might wonder if I ever felt second best, or as if Tony got all the girls and had all the fun. No. Tony gave me a great bit of the confidence I have today. When you get right down to it, he helped me to be comfortable around other people, not just girls. And, although I didn't adopt any of his "lines" or his M. O., I would be kidding myself if I ever thought I could have had half the experiences or become half the man I am, if I had not grown up with him. So we really did love each other like brothers. That's why this time, was probably the most difficult time we shared through our thirty years of knowing each other. Only later, through his illness, would the times become even tougher yet. Because this girl and I were such good friends, I was the guy that she told everything. That included the intimate details of her relationship with Tony. On the other side of the picture, I was Tony's closest friend.

Well, as often happens in relationships, theirs started to go on the rocks. She was becoming very clingy, and he was giving her the cold shoulder. I was on the receiving end of all her grief, and was getting angry for the way that Tony was treating my "friend girl". I had brought this up to him on several occasions, but to no avail. Finally, I went to the pool where he had probably already worked ten hours and was getting ready for a "Night swim." He was busy getting stuff ready, but I had to talk. "Tony, what's going on? She talked with me again for an hour. Why are you treating her like this? It's not like you." Tony let out a sigh and said: "You don't understand, stay out of it!" "She's my friend, and I don't like how you're treating her. She doesn't deserve that," I retorted. "What *does* she deserve then? Why don't *you* date her? Now let it go, it's not worth getting upset over." I responded: "Maybe that's the problem. I see a girl who's distraught because she feels like she's been dumped on, and you don't want to deal with it." He turned around and looked me in the eyes; I could tell he was getting angry. "Mike, let's discuss this later; I got a lot going on." "Let's discuss it now. I'm sorry it's not that convenient…"

3

"I'm sorry. I know this is not that convenient, but can you go with me? I don't know what I'm getting into. *Volleyball.*" His voice was raspy on the phone, like an old woman who's smoked for a hundred years. It sounded as though he had run a race, or at least done laps. I didn't know what I was getting into either, but responded on instinct: "You got it. You comin' down to get me?" "I'll be down in fifteen. Bring a weapon." Now I knew it was serious. He didn't go into any detail, I just knew the magic word. "*Volleyball.*" Sounds kinda weak for a code-word, but it worked. Tony and I had worked it out, so that if we were ever in a situation and needed back-up, that would be the word. No one would suspect it. He said he was going to get a shower and then meet me down here at my house, but I wasn't going to wait. I took my pellet gun that resembled a Beretta pistol, and tucked it in the back of my waistband. Whatever we were going to encounter, the gun *did* look real and perhaps could dissuade an attacker. I took a duffel bag that had my *chucks* and the sais for him, and I headed up to his house. His parents were away for the week visiting his sister out west, so he was home alone. It was convenient having his house less than a quarter mile behind mine. It was just a jog through three or four yards and I was at his back porch. The door was open, as was typical in Strasburg, so I walked in. I called out his name, but heard no reply. Now my concern was that the danger might be here, and that I better walk carefully.

I crept up his steps (turn of the century "L" shaped steps) leading up to the second floor with its six foot ceiling and bowed wooden floor. I walked slowly and carefully, trying not to drive a squeak from one of these ancient boards. I took a sharp right into his parents' room and although the rooms were dark, there was a faint light farther back, casting shadowy phantoms on the door and window. I took another right into an antechamber which used to serve as his own room. The white noise of the traffic on Main street and the flashing shadows made the room almost seem alive. Finally, his room was to the left, and I saw a shadow unlike the skittering phantoms caused by the racing headlights. The door was three-quarters of the way closed, so I walked toward it with every intention just to go on through, when Bam! The door slammed shut in my face, knocking me to the floor. I was certain my head had exploded, and that my brains and teeth now decorated the wood where a throw rug once was. The door had banged, but hadn't latched, so as it hit the door jamb it sprung back open only to reveal the silhouette of a towel-clad body holding a shotgun square on my head.

4

The kids were beginning to arrive at the swimming pool now. Tony was trying to get things ready for the "Night swim" but I was not going to let this "girl thing" rest. He let out a sigh of exasperation. "This is what's going on, but I don't expect you to understand. I just don't love her like that anymore. She's gotten too clingy; I mean she wants me to spend every friggin' moment with her, and I can't do it. I got work all day, and I want to hang out with my friends some of the time. She has friends, why can't she be with them? Haven't you ever had that problem? Can't you understand?" Well, I was beginning to have the problems, but the girl I was with at the time, was treating me, in a sense, the way Tony was treating this girl. The people at the pool were starting to line up for pizza and snacks. I could see Tony wanted to talk now, but he had other priorities that were pressing. I could relate part and parcel because of what this girl had done to me. Perhaps that's why it hit me so hard; who knows? That's something for the psychiatrists to figure out. The fact is, I was getting part of his story.

"Listen, if you want to fight over this… if you want to fight over a girl, that's fine; I'll fight. You've taught me every bit as much as I've taught you, and it'll probably be a pretty messy fight. But I think we're better than that. I think we're closer than that. Let's not let a girl come between what has taken us most of a lifetime up to this point to form. Blood is thicker…" I had forgotten about the blood. We were "blood brothers". I hadn't considered what was at stake until he said that. It was just a girl. She was a friend, mind you, but if it were any other guy I wouldn't interfere…and if it were just another of Tony's girlfriends, I wouldn't interfere. Why was this different? I would just have to deal with them as different people. I would love Tony, as Tony, and her, as her. I just looked at him and we both began to smile. It was shaky though…there was tension. "Okay." I said. "Come on and give us a kiss before they get here," (Tony quoting Mel Gibson in Lethal Weapon II.) and we embraced and that was it! The only fight we ever had…and over a girl. I wish I could say it was the only mess we had because of "his girls."

5

Tony lowered the gun. "Um…ouch! Are you a little jumpy or what? You didn't have to kick the door in my face, for the love of gussy." I was speaking like someone who was suffering from a bad cold. I carefully touched my nose, looking for the blood that follows such an impact. "I thought you were an intruder," he said with a laugh. "An intruder? An intruder? Come on Tone, I yelled your name." And the machine gun laugh began again. But it wasn't a full laugh. It wasn't a joyous one. It was a nervous laugh of someone who was trying to convince himself that he had nothing to be nervous about. It was the laugh of someone who is afraid of the dark, and is trying to convince themselves that there is no "boogie man" to be afraid of, during an impromptu blackout. He slipped on some jeans and a T-shirt that had *Steppenwolf* across the back. "Come on." We jumped in his Plymouth Barracuda and were off. "This is what's going on…" and the debriefing commenced.

6

"You remember her. Come on Mike, she was the one at the bowling alley." "Tony, there are many at the bowling alley." He tried to make a statement that would distinguish her from others. "You know; she's the pretty one with the long hair." "Oh yeah. I know her…and her twenty-eight sisters who look just like her. I mean really Tone, try and find something a little more unique, and don't make it anatomical; please spare me the details." "Well, you know her to see her, trust me. Anyway…" and he went on to relay the situation. She was at her house while her parents were on vacation. An ex-boyfriend had come to the house and was harassing her and throwing her around. There were no cell phones back then, so before this guy got into the house, she had called Tony. We were approaching the drive. It was a place I recognized, near the old Eagle Gun Museum, whatever that was. I really don't know much about it, but it had that bridge behind it that was always covered by the swelled waters of the Pequea creek. The guy's car was out in front of the house, and the front door was open. Obviously, he was no longer just outside.

I reached around and pulled out the gun. "Nice," Tony said. "I prefer something a little more intimidating." "What's more intimidating than a gun?" I remembered the one he had pointed at me just minutes ago. Yeah…where was that shotgun now? He opened up the large trunk of the Barracuda, that looked like the canopy on an F-14 Tomcat, and pulled out a baseball bat. Then I knew it was real. I mean, he did say "*Volleyball*" when he called. Now, there was no hesitation in his voice. "Let's go." We walked up to the house toward the door that was ajar. Immediately, we heard footsteps running across the wooden floor toward us. My heart was in my throat, and I started sweating (was it winter?). Tony backed up to the right of the door, ready to clock whoever came through. I was the lookout, and got into position by the door which was open, to identify the person running. I raised my left hand into the air by my head. That would give him the signal. My hand was open, as if asking a question in class, and yet, if we had a cease fire; if the person was the girl, I would make a fist and Tony would hold his position without hitting.

I pulled the Beretta up into position with my right hand, and the footsteps got extremely close. What would I do? Was I actually going to shoot this person? I mean, they were only pointed pellets, but one could do damage with that shot. I would shoot, and then Tony was gonna hit whatever came through that door. My hands tightened around the grip and the safety was flipped down. Tony was squeezing the grip on the bat and then loosening; squeezing, and loosening like a hitter ready to break the record. All I could see was the mottled shadowy wall and a silhouette fast approaching.

Finally, I got a visual. I made a fist in the air. And none too soon, as Tony was winding up for his record grand slam. I saw the blond hair sweeping around the corner. She didn't even see me, she was in such a hurry and running scared. As she passed Tony's position he grabbed her from behind, and turned her in a way so that as soon as she was caught, she would see who the captor was. She paused for a moment, unsure of who he was and why he was here. Then I came out of the shadows as well. She looked at him and started to sob, burying her face into his chest. "Okay, this is a great moment, and cinematographers would vie for such an authentic expression of relief, but isn't there a guy who is quite possibly dangerous somewhere in this house?" I wasn't much for heroics, but I did have a gift for sarcasm, and was not afraid to use it. They didn't get my humor, and I suppose if she had chosen my chest to rest on, I would not have wanted the disruption either, even though Tony clearly had no romantic interest in her at all. But it was a reality check, and both knew it to be true. Tony looked at her: "Go out in the car and lock the doors." "I called the police" she said. "They should be here at any time." Tony looked at me. "I want to take care of this. I don't want to leave any loose ends. This guy talks to the cops, and he can get out of it…he's a minor. He ain't getting out of it with us."

That was it. All she wrote. The girl got out of the house and ran to the Barracuda parked out in front. "You ready?" he said with determination in his voice. It was not so much a question as it was a prompt to go. "Ready? For what? What are we gonna do?" "Ready for anything. We have to take care of this one. It's gone too far. It's gone on for too long." "What do you mean 'take care of it'," I said. "I don't even know this guy and if he's some kind of 'whack-job' what are the odds he's gonna want to sit down and have a beer and talk about this?"

"I don't expect he'll want to talk. At least I hope not. You got my back." He wasn't asking. It was a statement. He wasn't smiling. "You have to ask?" I responded. We began to creep along the hallway; he with the bat resting on his right shoulder and me with the Beretta cocked and ready to go. What were we doing? Where were the cops?

CHAPTER EIGHTEEN

Disclosure

1

Few things can prepare you for some of the experiences you go through in life. And yet all the experiences contribute to it. They make us the persons we are, for better or for worse. I look on all my experiences as bricks within my foundation. Some have been weak or faulty, and yet the stronger ones hold the wall for those which cannot. Many hours, days and weeks can be spent worrying about something that may never happen. Many hours, days and weeks can be spent worrying about something that may only last for a few hours, days or weeks. At the beginning of teaching school that first year when I had decided to become a priest of the Diocese of Harrisburg, I had great anticipation for telling everyone what I was to do. I realized that I should not tell anyone, but still wanted to, more than ever. I remember it vividly.

2

I sat here today, having made my intentions known to many people who I care for very deeply, and who care for me as well, and was physically ill. I was shaking. I had spent many sleepless nights, worrying about how I would tell those that I love. Having told everyone, it is now out in the open, and I feel as though a building has been lifted from my shoulders. I feel "light as a feather," but also misunderstood. I think that the shock of this whole thing had not yet sunk in, but realize that abstract feelings and emotions cannot be expressed with words. "You my child, shall be called the prophet of the most high. For you will go before the Lord to prepare his way. To give his people knowledge of salvation by the forgiveness of sins." That quote is from the Canticle of Zechariah in Luke's Gospel. I love that line; because although it is certainly about Christ, it definitely speaks to me as the one who will "go before the Lord to prepare his way." Today I have taken the first step toward my life dedication to God. Many students asked if I would come back if the priesthood didn't work out. I know I will not be back. I am fulfilling my purpose… finally. We look so far around us to find out why we are here. We study many years and try many things to "find" ourselves, when all we really need to do is look to God. We need only ask.

3

"A teacher affects eternity. No one knows where his influence ends." I knew I had some influence as a teacher. This is witnessed even years later as I am in contact with some of my students and have witnessed weddings for some of them as well. But I am a product of such inspirations as well. And as I take this look back on my life, and look at all of the people who have most been a part of it, I see pictures in my mind of my parents, brothers and sisters, aunts and uncles;

grandparents, friends and teachers. There is this "collage" of relatives and close friends that is a picturesque summary of my life and times both good and bad. Toward the last quarter of this collage, there is an abrupt transition. There was a break in the smooth continuity that existed since my birth. This break stands only to accentuate that part of my life, in which a change occurred due to a positive figure entering my life at that time. An individual who would continue to influence me, even after graduation, and hence for the rest of my life.

A sophomore at Shippensburg University in the fall of 1992, I was still in my high school mode, and was very reserved in using all of the resources available by the University. I was still dabbling with osteology, which I had begun to explore in high school, and was looking for bigger and better ways to do things. I had approached many professors with questions regarding skeletons and articulation of them, and few gave me the time of day. I was referred to this figure known only to me as "Dr. Kirkland," or "Kirkland." This name would come up every time I mentioned questions I had about skeletons and the like. I decided to locate this professor, and give it a last chance. I am glad I did.

As I approached his office, a myriad of signs and bumper stickers littered the window, which kept me from getting a sneak peak at this guy, who was becoming more intriguing by the minute. Office hours were posted on the door, and I had come at a time outside of these hours. It so happened that all of the hours coincided with times that I had classes or other commitments. The sign read: "If not in here, in room 228." Obviously that was his research lab, I thought. Later, I would find out that this guy had two offices.

Early in the week, I was on my way to my first class of the day, which incidentally was in the afternoon, and saw his door cracked open so that just a sliver of light shone through. My heart started beating faster, and my palms started to get sweaty. This was it. I was finally going to meet this guy that, up to this point, I had only heard about. I had seen no pictures of him, nor had I heard anything from students regarding him. This was an exercise in confidence. This was an exercise in faith. What would I see? How would he react? Would this be another slap in the face? I approached the door and listened. Not a sound came out… but wait. There was a slight sound; A whining almost. The sound was like the strings of violins. As I moved closer to the partially open door, no longer was it simply a humming, but now I could make out the faint sound of many violins. Vivaldi! This professor was listening to Vivaldi in his office. The sweet sound filled the air, and calmed my heart and sweaty palms. I decided that I would count to eight, and then knock. If no one answered, I would try back another time. One. I was thinking about the track record that I had racked up so far. Two. Maybe this "bone thing" wasn't worth all of the energy that I was putting into it. Three. Four. What am I worried about? If he is not interested, then he is not interested. Five. It's not like he's going to bite my head off or anything. Six. What if I just called and left a message. Seven. I'll just tr… fweee. I never got to eight.

4

We were now creeping down the hallway. He had the bat cocked and ready to go, while I held the beretta toward the floor. "I've always backed you up…I ain't gonna stop now." Why did he keep looking back at me? Did he think I was going to turn tail and run? Well, if he did, he wouldn't have been too far from the truth. I was on the verge of calling the whole thing off. "Shouldn't we let those who were trained for this stuff do this stuff?" We began down the hallway from the kitchen to the living room. Lights were on all over the place, but there was no one here. That was the scary part. This guy was obviously hiding. We had a ball bat and a gun that shot little lead pellets. What were we going to do? Tony put his fist in the air, to stop me in my tracks. The room opened up to a stairway off the living room. I stopped in my position and he looked towards the stairs. There were no lights on up there, and I knew beyond any doubt, up those stairs was where we were headed.

5

I was a bio-osteologist. Dr. Kirkland paved the way for this. (Look for my book to come out sometime in the near future "Skeletry: Art and Articulation.") I put animal skeletons together and sold them across the country. You will find my skeletons in many of the zoos and museums across the United States and Canada; even some places in Europe. Some of my students gloried in their ability to share in the process. I had one student, who would go on to become a physician's assistant because of her experiences in helping me to dissect and assemble the skeletons. Brittany really had a gift for that. Another would go on to become a nurse, and let me assure you, she had the cleanest dissections and study skins I have ever seen, but I digress. I had it all, it would seem. I had used my gifts and abilities and had never wanted for anything...except for this. Yep, I had it all... seemingly, and yet something was missing.

So I found myself studying to be a priest. Catholics believe that the priest is a man called by God to be their spiritual leader. There will be many arguments that there is no need for an intermediary between God and man. Well, I could be wrong, but throughout time God called...um Noah...Abraham...Israel...Moses...the prophets, et alia. We believe that he continues to call his priests to be His representative before the people, and their representative before God. This is the vocational call I had been running from for so long and now was answering in a very real way.

Now don't get me wrong, this was of no surprise to me. I was called at an early age. When one is called and when one answers, are two very different distinct things. I love my life. It wasn't always that way. I have found that when I am close to God, and responding to His plans, I am most happy and content. Nothing is missing. These times most often are when I have little to no distractions in my life. When nothing separates the connection between us I have an inner calm; an inner peace. This is a satisfaction that no money or material possessions can give. This feeling is like a drug that you can never get enough of; and so you crave it and want more and more. The more you get, the more you want, until it absorbs your whole life. This is what I felt and this is why I had been driven to make that decision. If everyone knew what it was like to feel this, there would be no shortage of Christians in this world. On the contrary people would be breaking down the doors to become religious, because they would realize that this is the single most awesome feeling in the world; this is the only feeling in the world; this is the one thing that everyone seeks, but many do not find. This IS the one thing that everyone seeks… but few can find. Few can find it because it is hidden among the many distractions of life. "…It is easier for a camel to pass through the eye of a needle, than for a rich man to enter the kingdom of Heaven…" We are seldom happy if we are not doing the will of God.

6

Tony was halfway up the stairs of the girl's house when he raised his hand again. He bent his fingers at the knuckle, giving the sign to come ahead. We had no flashlight, and it was dark up there, but it seemed Tony would not be reluctant to ruin the darkness with a touch of the switch. He was different tonight. There was something in the air. I don't know whether it was adrenaline or testosterone, but he was driven and would not be satisfied coming out of this house empty-handed. I walked over to the stairs and began my ascent. I stayed on the stairs, probably half scared and the other half, just watching his back. He began his trek down the hallway. There were three bedrooms and a bathroom. There were two doors on the left, which was the back of the house, and one on the right. The door to the bathroom at the end of the hall was open. He began walking towards it and gave me the high sign to come with him. The other three doors were closed, so we decided to check the bathroom first, and then double back and clear the other rooms. It was easy to be quiet, even in this old house, because of the carpet and the noise of traffic outside. We entered the bathroom, looking in the shower and in the linen closet. There was no one, and nothing that would indicate someone had been here. We turned off the light and began back down the hallway.

The master bedroom was to the left now, or so we presumed. We opened the door like a "bull in a china shop," making enough noise to raise the dead. Tony flicked on the light and we scanned the place. We approached the closet, and my heart started beating again heavily in my chest. I walked over to the window and peered out at Tony's car. The engine was running and she was still inside. Tony grabbed the closet door with his right hand and backed against the hinges so he would be behind the door when it opened. I lifted the Beretta once again and fixed it on the door. It was a quick count of "three" and he opened the door. There was nothing but some clothes and a set of golf clubs. We had cleared the room, so we turned out the light and entered the hallway. The air was cold, and we felt the chill. Once again, our hearts began to beat loudly. The two bedroom doors facing us were now open.

7

The office door swung open and "Kirkland" (I presumed) was on his way out. He stopped abruptly, and he looked startled. "Oh!" he said. "Hello." I just stood there looking. I had rehearsed many times what I would say, and was all set to say it and nothing came out. He looked at me, as though I were the latest escapee off the turnip truck, but said nothing. Dr. Kirkland was about five foot ten, and one hundred, sixty pounds. He had a "flattop buzz" looking kind of haircut, and was wearing glasses. He had on a plaid shirt and blue jeans. On his head was a contraption, which looked like a cross between an "old-time doctor's" reflective head mirror, and a visor from "Robo-cop," or "Star trek." His hair was peppered with gray, and his face cleanly shaven. He must have followed my gaze, because he quickly reached up and removed the visor, and then asked; "May I help you?" Help me he did.

Dr. Kirkland, or Dr. "K" as he was affectionately called, molded me over the next three years into the person I am today. Although I never had him as a professor for a single class, he taught me more outside of the classroom, than I could ever have learned in a lecture hall or lab. He summed it all up, however, in three precepts that have stayed with me, and will continue to stay with me until I die.

Precept number one was this: "Do not try to be anything but that which you are; and be that perfectly." I was a scientist. But he had the sight to see past that. He saw me as something different from other biologists. He saw a drive toward my work with bones, and initiative. Because of these, he was constantly encouraging me to do better. He would not accept anything less than the best. I remember him, once, watching me make up a study skin. A study skin is formed when an animal specimen is skinned, and the skin stuffed with cotton, and formed into proper anatomical position. At the time, I looked at this particular skin as my crowning achievement as a museum employee. I had taken a lot of time and effort in making sure everything was perfect. When making a study skin, the mount could not just have a nose; it had to be a pointy nose, and could not just have a butt; it had to be a squared off butt. Dr. Kirkland was very clear with respect to how things were to be done. I remembered showing him the skin after it had dried and will never forget his reply. He simply said: "That's pretty good for a beginning mount. Now let's see a good one." He then showed me what was wrong with the one that I had in my hand. I was humbled. I had a good lesson in humility that day. I knew that there were other study skins that were much worse than the one I had done, but also knew that I could do better. I was proud before I had reason to be. In the future months and years, I received much praise from Dr. Kirkland, and accepted it graciously. I knew that Dr. Kirkland really meant any compliment he gave, for he wanted me to be the best I could be… and then be better.

The second precept he gave me was: "Always make time for the important things in your life. If you don't make time, you will never have time." I had found myself at times rushing aimlessly through my days to get things done that had to be done. I had lessened recreational activities at one point, and really had no "down time." Dr. Kirkland was constantly reminding me that life was not all about work. Life was not all about getting one thing done so you could move to another. Life was about *living*. Take time to watch the train. Take time and stop to check roadkills. Take the time to enjoy the nature that we spend so much time studying. This was the hardest precept for me, but I have learned to live by it as much as possible.

The third precept and, by far, one of the most important was: "If you can get paid doing what you love to do the most, you are the luckiest man alive." When he said that, it seemed to make a lot of sense. Actors, athletes, and stars must be the happiest people alive right? I didn't understand this quote at all. Only years later when I began to teach did this quote finally make sense. I assumed that normal people didn't like their jobs. Not that they hated them, but it was something that they *had* to do. As a teacher, I was getting paid doing what I loved to do, and affecting the lives of hundreds. What more could one want.

8

I visited Dr. Kirkland early in the year. He had been fighting cancer for many months with many different treatments. I made him a bat skeleton as a Christmas gift and finally had the chance to get it to him. Dr. Kirkland was a self made man. He answered to no one because he was usually right, and was in charge of the situation. When I visited him on that day in January we spoke for about an hour, and I said "I am lucky." I recalled what he had said to me so many years ago in "Precept Three." "Where else can you get paid to have so much fun?" I was referring to teaching. He stopped me, and reached on the floor where a yellow legal pad lay. He picked it up and paged through and he read: "Riding home on my bike, I now realize what Lou Gherig meant when he said: 'Today I am the luckiest man alive.' I have a loving wife, a wonderful son, and a career that I love. How many others can claim as much?" He wept.

I didn't know that Dr. Kirkland *could* cry. That moment changed me forever. He was scared, but helped me to realize what *is* most important in life. That brought me to a new precept that would cover all of the other three previously mentioned. "People are the most important thing. People are what really matter." Dr. Kirkland died Monday, 15 February 1999, due to organ failure as the melanoma took over his body. His body died; his spirit lives on.

9

What humbled me in my twenties was that Tony really fell into his faith. See, Dr. Kirkland, as much of a scientist as he was, taught me about that too. I saw Tony exhibiting these principles and he didn't even know it. Don't get me wrong, he was always religious. What I mean by "fell into his faith" is, that he had a deep faith and respect for God, but he didn't go to church or really practice his faith that way.

Now… he is a staunch Methodist. Go figure…a Roman Catholic and a Methodist: best friends. Need I mention that, at one point, I was the first Roman Catholic President of the Methodist Church Youth Group in Strasburg. The first and last, and did not formally defect from my own religion. It was amazing how much they wanted to know about my faith. Talk about Ecumenism. But Tony became involved. Even to this day, he teaches Sunday school and has adult groups he meets with. I am so pleased at how he's done so much for his Church. I think that his wife played no small part in that as well. But it was interesting how he was really going on a good course.

When I told him I was going to become a priest (and he was the first one I told), I don't think he really understood the implications. We had always had this plan to one day open a bar together at Key West. He would be the bouncer and I would be the bartender. We had plans, but some of those were foregone because he was married and had kids. I too, would be married now, but it would be different. He would still support me now, unconditionally, as I had supported him in the past.

I had discovered, since I made the decision to finally go through the process to become a priest, that there were miracles everywhere in my life. These little miracles and signs were all around me, if I just stopped and observed. My miracle this particular week was that I didn't pass out when I told my fellow teachers about my intentions. I was physically ill and shaking all over. I am not a nervous person, and I will remember this day forever simply for the fact that I was nervously shaking for the first time in my life. Most of the students had said congratulations, which translated to me meant, "This is what he would want to hear." Some people were really sincere, while others were holding back the regret in their voice. We can lie with words, but our bodies tell a different story. I left school that day, a million tons lighter, and had a beer. The hardest part was yet to come.

CHAPTER 19

A Bad Day

1

This was just not turning out to be a good day. What were we going to do now? The two doors were ajar, and there was cold air coming in through the windows. What were the odds that we were going to get out of this unscathed? "What do you want to do?" I had been waiting for him to ask that question. I had to be careful with my choice of words, because if Tony thought I was "chickening out", or giving us an excuse to leave, he would insist on clearing the rooms. "Tone, the cops are gonna be here any minute. Let's let them handle it. She's out there now, and probably already freakin' out wondering if we're dead or alive. All she's seen is lights going on and off." "Damn" he said, and there was no levity in it. He was mad. "Tone, let's just go. Let's take care of her and we'll take care of this guy another time." That was it. A sigh of relief escaped my lips as we reached the stairs and began our descent. All was fine now. The cops would arrive and we would put her in their hands. They could check out the house and we could go home. Tony reached the bottom of the stairs and I was about half way down when we heard it. It was only a whisper, coming from the upstairs: "Tooooonyyyy. Tonnnnyyy." It was a mocking whisper of one who had won the day. We froze. Our eyes met, and I gently moved my head from left to right and back again, as if to say: "It's not worth it. Let's go." We continued down the stairs backwards, waiting for the attack. It never came. We went out to the car and drove with her to a friend's house. We dropped her off there, and she called the cops again. We headed back to Strasburg, doubling back by the house. His car was gone.

2

It was a gift for me to teach. I have to admit, sometimes even now, when I frequent the school, it is a selfish act, because they bring with them so much energy and love. It's addictive. The week was Catholic School's week; two weeks after I had made my intentions known to the school. This week was one of the best planned and most enjoyable events that our school experienced, both as teachers and students. When told about the activities, it appeared as though the week would be a nice break because while activities are going on, we don't usually teach the students during that time. It appeared as though I might have had a little more free time that week than I normally did. Appearances, however, are often deceiving.

For whatever reason, that week seemed endless. It felt as though I was working twice as hard to do half of the teaching I normally do. I was running around trying to accomplish things that probably should have been done earlier and getting bent out of shape because things were not easier. As always at this time of year, Science Fair was going on, and I required so much from the students, that I was constantly proofreading, or correcting some component of their projects. I also had labs to set up, and was trying to get paperwork in for the deadline on my diocesan application.

On another level, some students were becoming problematic in that their usually tolerable behavior was going over the boundaries. I loved all of my students dearly, and tried to be empathetic to their issues and quirks in life. Perhaps it was the stress, or the fact that I was not feeling up to par, but things were bothering me a lot more than usual. I wasn't myself. I often found myself that week more concerned about whether or not the students were being quiet, and not so concerned about whether or not they were enjoying the week and learning something.

I attended a dinner on Wednesday of that week to honor Catholic school teachers, and at that dinner, they were giving out awards for different attributes teachers had. When it was time to give out the award for the most creative, I had my doubts it would be me, however, in the introduction to this award, the announcer mentioned some teacher's ability to take anything like "roadkill" and string it together to be creative, among other things. At this point, I knew it was me he was referring to. I was the only one in the room; in the state; that would have roadkill associated with his name.

I waited with growing anticipation as the master of ceremonies listed yet more qualities of a creative teacher, mixed with some facetiousness. Finally, he began to announce the winners from each of the schools, and I waited with nervous tension, and was rehearsing how I would act when called upon to receive my award. Would I smile graciously, or run up to get the prize, or would I act shy and surprised by their decision. I was waiting for the curtain call that would never come. When the announcement came, my heart sank. Someone else was called. It was not me to whom he was referring, even though he mentioned that word which had been associated with me for the last five years previous to teaching. To this day I still don't know why he included "roadkill" in the litany of attributes. I clapped of course, but was deeply disappointed. I did win an award for faculty peacemaker, but it didn't hold the same meaning. I worked so hard to make science something the kids wanted to be a part of. I worked so hard to make something no one else could make. I worked so hard to be creative.

I thought about the woman who won. I thought for a long time. She was in school as much as I was, if not more. She was the most upbeat person I knew, all of the time. She maintained a smile amidst crying children, unforeseen misfortunes, and lessons gone awry, and could always pull something out of it. The children were drawn to her in a way that I had never seen with a teacher, and the word new or innovative, was commonplace for her. She was a creative mastermind. She was deserving of more than some gag gift for creativity; for she had something more than I did. Not only did she have this creative genius and the dedication and drive to implement these ideas, but also she would stop whatever she was doing and take the time to chat. She would pause in the midst of work, to share a joke or funny story. She could laugh at lessons gone badly, and put aside her "time" for the sake of the children, while also being a wife and mother.

3

I had since forgotten my pride. I was humbled, and it took that experience to humble me. And at the end of the week, I thought to myself, "If I can just get through Friday, the weekend would bring rest". "Home Free," as Tony would say. I was working in the lab on correcting science fair papers vigorously, so that the students could have their rough drafts to work on over the weekend. I heard a tiny knock at the door. I didn't get up to get it, because I was so intent on finishing these papers, and figured if they really need something they'll just walk in. The knock came again, and I was becoming irritated. I was tired, stressed, and behind, and the last thing I wanted to do was talk to someone else.

The door opened, and a young girl walked into the lab. She left the door open for a moment, and then reached over and grabbed the handle and gently closed the door. She was maybe six or seven years old and her hair was neatly pulled back so that some hit her shoulders. A timid smile lit up her face and she stood there shyly, looking across the room at me with her intuitive eyes. Often times in the teaching profession, students are used as messengers, or errand runners, and I accepted this as simply that; a messenger with something for me. A messenger she was, but not the kind I had expected.

I just wanted to take whatever she had to deliver, and get back to work. I was intent on finishing these papers. I looked up at her. "Yes?" She began to walk slowly toward me and as she did, she replied, "I have something for you." She walked over to me where I was. As I was sitting, she was standing beside the desk and we were now eye to eye. She looked at me with her shy smile and said: "I finished my first rosary today, and I want you to have it." I lost all sense of where I was and what I was doing for what seemed like forever, and then looked down into her innocent eyes and felt ashamed. Who was I that this little flower was giving me something that she considered very precious? How was it that this young girl deemed me worthy of such a wonderful treasure?

I smiled, and the words "thank you" stumbled from my trembling lips. I thanked her and said how wonderful it was, but on the inside I was crying. I thanked her again and quickly lead her out of the lab and into the school. I then returned to the lab where I wept. I could hold it no longer. I didn't know why I was crying, for this girl had certainly honored me with this gift. I didn't even have her as a student, and she was honoring me. I realized that I was becoming the teacher I had always hoped I would never become. I realized that I was becoming so concerned with the details and the material, that I was ignoring the most important part of teaching… the students. The reason I entered teaching in the first place was that I wanted to make a difference, and show students that they were the most important things.

That Friday, I made a big step. I realized that a change must occur. People are the most important; everything else is just details. I needed to put my priorities in order, and stop letting details shape my attitude toward life. That third precept that Dr. Kirkland had taught me years before was bearing fruit. I count this little flower's rosary among my most valuable possessions; priceless in my eyes. She gave me a treasure which was much better than any certificate.

4

I have been fortunate as of late, that when I have asked God for help, He has graciously given to me. He continues to give me what I need, and yet sometimes I am afraid. Because "of those to whom much is given…much is expected." I wondered what He might take some day. I think I have a better understanding now, than I did when that little girl offered me a part of her life. It's funny how God works…even through the "little ones;" especially through the "little ones." When I needed Him most, He knocked on the door. I chose not to answer it, so He knocked again. I thank Him with all my heart that He decided not to try knocking again, but to simply walk in and answer my prayer. And I thank you, Alexandra, as well.

CHAPTER TWENTY

The Brilliant Idiot

1

"My butt still hurts from your bike tire." "What?" "You remember: I wanted to ride your bike, because I didn't have mine down at your place, and you were riding around me in circles, mocking me." "You were so easy to mock." We reached another corner and were readying ourselves for the corner kick. "Ladies and gentlemen, there's the kick… it's up…it's…it's…oh my he did it! Double point bounce on the corner, unbelievable." "Now the other kick is up;" "I don't know Johnny, looks like a back-spin on that one." "We've seen Mike put that spin on now and again, and this might be an awful risk. He's trailing by three. It's up…going…and yes! Got the two points, but that's it." We were doing our own commentary, and the night was getting late. We recalled that back then, Tony had this metal pipe about the size of a small sword, and he kept it with him. It was just an old metal pipe, but still pretty solid. I was riding my bike around him in tight circles. I made larger and larger circles as my mockery of him continued. While I was riding all of a sudden, he threw the pole at the front tire of my bike, and it slid through the spokes locking the wheel against the forks and tossing me over the handlebars into the street. He seemed to feel kind of bad, until I got up with only a few scrapes. He immediately grabbed the bike and began to ride.

2

My bike, "Tempest" by name, was no ordinary bike. Then again, most of the things I had were modified in some way; thus, the grappling hook shooter that got me into this reflection. Later on in my high school years, my first car would be modified into a "Knight Rider" version of the Subaru. I had replaced the normal console in the front with a command center. My steering wheel was one I had modified from the junk yard. I had taken a regular wheel from an old Chevy, and cut off the top semi-circle of the wheel and the bottom semi-circle of the wheel, so that it looked like an airplane steering wheel. I then took some old bike grips, and put them over the two handles on either side. Underneath these grips I ran the wiring to the two buttons that operated the missile launchers. I know; you're thinking, "Come on!" but it's true. I can't imagine, in this day and age of terrorism and school shootings, what kind of trouble I could've gotten into, because I showed this stuff to my friends and fellow students. I guess they just knew that I wasn't a bad kid. I know there are some kids I went to high school with who saw these things and were in disbelief as well. I had mounted two PVC pipes on the arm of my *Armitron* robot arm in the hatchback of my vehicle. The pipes had a protractor on the side to get the angle right. The missiles were model rockets, that were loaded in on a rod sticking up within the tubes, and their fuses were connected to the alligator clips that ran to the steering wheel. I would do future experiments as a teacher…just ask my students I had in seventh and eighth grade about the rocket engine volcanoes, or our tests with velocity and acceleration using their toy cars.

To activate the circuit, it was necessary to flip four switches on the console. The buttons on the steering wheel would light up, showing that they were ready for launch. I also wanted to have an oil slick, but didn't know how to work that, until I saw my dad using the poison pump sprayer. I took the pump sprayer and widened the nozzle because the oil was so thick. The oil did come out of the hose when pressurized. I ran the tube through the back of the car, where the license plate lights came through. I pumped the tank and then had a wire cable attached to a plunger button, like a syringe in the front. When I pressed the button, the trigger on the pump would compress and out came the oil. Although I never got to use it, it was pretty cool to have. Finally, I wanted a license plate changer. I had seen in it a movie. My dad collected old license plates, so that wasn't a problem. After I put them onto a three sided cylinder and attached a little motor which would rotate them; I had to figure out how to mount them on the car. Well, I could have cut the back end of the car, because the license plate was on the car and not the bumper. I never did end up attaching it, for the obvious reasons. But the rockets did fire in a field by Lampeter-Strasburg High School.

I made slight modifications to *Tempest* as well. I had a command center over the handlebars, with a walkie-talkie attached. There was a small super-soaker like gun mounted on the top. But the most unique feature of my bike was the "anti-theft" system. I had removed the banana seat and replaced it with a smaller seat. As I did this, I modified the shaft into which the seat post was inserted with a compression spring. The seat was put to my level to ride and the spring compressed. If anyone heavier than I sat on the bike, the lock would release and when the weight was removed, the seat would fly off of the bike. I was constantly inventing new things.

3

"I told you. But you didn't believe me; you just wouldn't let up. You deserved that one." And he began that laugh. But the joke was on him. I just watched as he rode the bike around me, as I had ridden around him only moments before. He had sat down on the seat. That would be a fatal mistake. I watched, just waiting to see the anti-theft system in action, but he wouldn't stand up to pedal. He obviously needed motivation. I picked up the bar and acted as if I were going to avenge myself, using his own weapon against him. He stood up to pedal faster and farther away from me and in an instant, the seat flew into the air. It had worked! But he didn't know anything had happened, until all of a sudden he sat down and "Rrrrpppppt." His rump had made contact with the spinning rear wheel. It sounded like a semi rolling over the rumple strips on the turnpike exits. I saw him leap up from that position like he had sat on hot coals. I couldn't contain myself…I just started to laugh. Half out of the comic vengeance and half out of the surprise of success!

CHAPTER TWENTY-ONE

Of all the colors of the Rainbow,
I have grown quite fond of Blue

1

"That still hurts. I got scars." "Please. Not half the scars I have from my own inventions." Not all scars are bad though. Scars can leave us not only with pain, but with experience. Something that makes us better, or want to be better. If we can't find meaning in the pain, then there's just pain. But if we can get something from it…if we can take these pains and reflect on them and the relevance in our life now…wow. I include these stories about teaching, because they really shaped the person I would become. But in a greater way, and perhaps ironically, all those things I did for the students…all that they saw in me…I saw in Tony…I received from him.

2

My person is a composite of many. I reflect back on my life, and it is a mosaic of experiences, people, trials, and victories that have made me who I am becoming. I have already expounded on some of my "kids" and the various antics and situations that have transpired over the years. But I would be remiss if I didn't dedicate a chapter to one such soul who has left footprints on my heart; fingerprints on my mind; and a picture of what it is to love. This chapter isn't for me necessarily, nor is it for you, although you may continue to read if the spirit moves you. This chapter is for her, for there are symbols, experiences, and nuances that only she will understand, having lived them.

"The influence of a teacher is endless; no one can ever tell where it ends." Often, people ask how I could ever want to give up having children in order to pursue the vocation to the priesthood. My response may sound cliché, but it is the truth. I have more "kids" than would ever be possible for me within the Sacrament of Marriage. There is no other way to put it. In my brief experience as a teacher, I have had in excess of five hundred kids. I love them all; feel their pains; see their victories; and experience their trials. They are "my kids." I honestly cannot think of a time when I have not loved teaching. Some might say "You obviously didn't teach then," or "You must have let the kids walk all over you." Neither is further from the truth. At the risk of sounding vain, I will say that my students truly loved me, and I loved them. I say that not for the sake of vanity, but to demonstrate a point. The reason we have many problems in the schools today is that some of those who teach have stopped loving the kids, and have accepted the life of a teacher as a nine to five position. Some of the parents have stopped raising their children, and are satisfied with having a friend.

As a teacher, I worked very hard: not to impress people, or impress myself (well most of the time), but so that my kids would enjoy school, and love to be there. That is not to say that some did not like to be in my class, but that I put forth an effort so that many could flourish. Three words have stuck with me since my teacher training days and have guided me on my way to becoming an excellent teacher. Be fair, firm, and consistent. These are easy words to say, but difficult words to uphold. I like to think that I was a tough teacher, in that I expected my students to have to study and work to achieve good grades and feel confident. I also like to think I was fair, in that I treated all kids in the way that was fair to them, based on their attributes, and abilities. That doesn't mean everyone was treated the same, but everyone was treated fairly. The consistency was the tough part for me, because it was hard for me to be consistent, when I was so scatter-brained. I still work on that today, and it is just as hard as it always was.

Of all the things I offered the kids, though, the curriculum was not the most valuable. My love was the greatest gift I could offer; and most accepted that gift with open arms. For teachers, to touch a child these days is a deadly exercise. We all walk around on pins and needles and hope we won't get sued…. or shot. My whole attitude was one of the *Good*. I never second-guessed my movements, actions, or words, because they were always toward the good and for the children. Those who second-guess their actions probably shouldn't be making actions at all. I believe it was this openness, and willingness to open my heart to them, which allowed them to let their guard down, and open their lives to me. And from this, I have gained treasure far more valuable than any material possession. I truly am a father / mother / brother / sister / friend, and I wouldn't trade it for the world. I love, and am in love, with multitudes of people, who make up my family. What a wonderful gift I have been given, and so as with any wonderful gift I am given, I care for it as though it were my only possession.

In school, my favorite times of day were homeroom, recess, and after school. Although I treasured the times in the classroom when I got to share my religion, science, and English knowledge, the times before and after school were times when the kids would sit and tell me about their lives. They shared their secrets, dreams, worries, and invited me into their lives for just a little while each day. These were not always the most pleasant experiences.

3

We continued to kick the ball back and forth across the path we had taken so many times before. But this time was different. I wondered if I would ever do this again. "Things are gonna change you know." Tony said. "I doubt we'll be able to play foosball once you get your church." "Yeah." I said with a certain sadness. It wasn't a sadness of depression as much as it was saying goodbye to an old life...an old friend, and welcoming a new one. "Lots of things are going to change." "Well, people change Tone. I mean look at you! Look at me! We're the poster boys for change." He laughed. People do change, I learned this from Mandy.

4

I was a science teacher before entering the seminary. One year I had an eighth grade student named Mandy. Now Mandy was cantankerous. She had such a negative attitude about everything in life and at the source of her hardship was me, her teacher. Everything was my fault and she had no qualms about informing me of that daily. Finally, she graduated from eighth grade. I left for the seminary but she and I didn't communicate as many students did with me over the next five years. My last year in seminary I was struggling with the issue of change. I wondered after speaking to thousands of people who seemed "stuck" if people *could* change. I was really struggling with this question. Mandy's brother contacted me and said she was in the hospital and it seemed serious. I found myself on the way to the hospital to visit thinking: What makes me think she would want any visitors, let alone *ME;* the one who seemed to be the source of so many of her problems. I entered the hospital room. She was alone. She could not speak nor open her eyes. I walked in and said: "Mandy, it's Mr. Rothan"...and she smiled. Over the next month, I visited her four other times and each time she improved. She now had her eyes open but still could not speak.

I reflected that I was about to be ordained a deacon and yet during all these visits, not once did I offer to pray with her. Not once! I was worried that maybe she would say no, or do it begrudgingly, but this last time I was determined to pray. Her eyes were open this last visit, but she could not speak and as I entered the room the nurse said: "Don't touch her. We have wires and monitors and everything set up, so don't mess it up!" Finally as my visit was concluding I got up the courage and said: "Mandy, I would like to pray with you now, but the nurse said......." And she reached up and grabbed my hand. And I prayed the hardest prayer I ever prayed. I got up and kissed her on her head. And as I left that room I *knew,* PEOPLE COULD CHANGE. Through suffering, Mandy had undergone a transformation. The woman I saw before me, had no remnant of the girl I once knew, left within her. And at the end of her life, the words, "I love you" rolled very easily from her lips.

5

Death is a part of every life. I mean let's face it, we're all dying from a disease called mortality. Tony came to the golf course. I was working the evening shift and I noticed that some of the older girls were crying. My first thought was that it was some kind of high school drama. I could count on one hand all the times Tony actually came to my work while I was working. I knew it must be important. His friend from school had just died in a car accident. I couldn't believe it. I knew the kid from being around the pool and just hanging out with Tony. He was one of our own. He was our age! Now he was gone. We often experience little deaths in this life to prepare us for the final death. This was no small incident, but I noticed a change in both of us from that point forward. It was an eerie feeling. For perhaps for the first time, we realized we were mortal...we were not invincible. That truth realized, would affect how we acted from that point forward. It kind of forced us to grow up; and that would be important for what we were to face further down the road.

6

The times when I was a teacher I savor. They were high points in my life. I remember in particular that recess at school was a release for *me*. It was a time when I could play again and no one would bat an eye because I was with my kids. For someone to invite you into their life takes a great deal of trust and humility.

I was a twenty-four-year-old male science teacher. I was in a classroom with thirteen and fourteen-year-old girls and boys, and didn't think twice at times when they would give me a hug or drop me a note. When they would ask me questions about myself, or my life, and tell me things about theirs, I couldn't judge them, or turn them off. They were / are truly my kids. Now as they grow up, I see them going through changes. Many are moving in positive directions, and many in the opposite direction. Some have remained clear in their goals, while others don't know what they're doing, or where they're going. Some have gone down hill, and others went through trials and failures to rise once again to the top. I still can't judge them, and recess is over, but I have remained open to them, and they continue to open up to me. I am truly a father of many, and love them all dearly. Some will continue to go on their prodigal journeys, and others will always remain close at home; but either way, they all know they will always have a warm safe home in my heart. God bless my kids, as he has blessed me with their love.

Names are unimportant when it is principles one wishes to get across, so for all practical purposes, I will call her "Blue." I met her, my first year teaching middle school and thought she might prove a bit of a challenge. I had known her father only a few weeks before meeting her, and so thought she might "have something to prove." As I would later find out, it was I who had something to prove, and she would provide a model that I could reflect on for years to come. She was a typical teenager (that is not meant to be delimiting or diminutive). Most of our conversations occurred after school when she would be waiting around and gain access to my homeroom, along with another at times just to talk. It was then that I got to know these kids the most....after school. She was totally taken by this boy, who was probably a year younger, and although he often provided material for light conversation, he always opened the door to topics that were deeper than grade school sweethearts. He often provided the handle for the doorway to the soul.

7

Thinking back on those times, especially in the climate that is looming currently, I sometimes cringe at how trusting I was, and at the risks I took. It may have been a bit of naiveté, however, the kids always responded well. I gave them my email (and I was new to this "email thing" at the time.) Some used it for questions and the like, but there was one who wrote often about issues that really lay heavily on the heart. Things that kids shouldn't have to deal with, but did, and I was happy to be invited, if even briefly, into their world. This particular girl "Blue" wrote almost daily, and at first I figured it was probably a typical "grade school crush." Further emails proved to go beyond a superficial understanding, and there was a bond of confidence created. For really the first time in my life, I had kids talking to me, under confidentiality, and baring their souls because they had found "someone who listens." For the first time in a really long time in my life, I felt fulfilled; but that was about to change abruptly.

One of the difficulties in writing a book about your life, is that you run into so many people who have made an impact, but those times they made the greatest impact happened to be times they were also confiding in me. Therefore, for me to share what they said, even if their names are not known, would be to do violence to the confidence I promised, so I will do the best I can to talk around the issues.

I was called into the principal's office (that hadn't happened since high school) and she was inquiring about one of my students. She had heard I was emailing and knew that the students confided in me. She asked me about a rumor she had heard regarding two students. The rumor involved this student "Blue" to whom I had given my word of confidence unless what she told me was criminal, or detrimental to her safety or that of her classmates. Therefore, I exercised something I would only learn later in seminary to be an actual phenomenon. I exercised "mental restraint." This concept is given to the question of whether or not you are obliged to tell the truth to someone who has no right to hear it, and the answer is no. If I shared what this student had spoken with me about, it would have done nothing to contribute to the betterment of the school or the students. Therefore I kept confidence. That's one thing I have been able to maintain over the years of hearing thousands of stories. For someone to let you into their world, requires a certain degree of integrity and a greater degree of amnesia.

When I was a teacher I knew nothing of *mental restraint*, but I said I couldn't share anything at that time. Could I be liable for this? Perhaps.

Was it worth losing the trust of someone who was totally vulnerable? Absolutely not. Another teacher was called in who also contacted the kids at times, and she told what she knew. The next morning, I received an email from the student and it just ruined my whole weekend. It was my first year teaching these kids and they didn't really know me. I felt like I was starting to get in the door and really get close to them (which is always a risk), and then I read the e-mail. At first my heart just felt heavy, and I got one of those lumps in my throat. I can't say what was in the email, but all in all she thought I had betrayed her, and I was wondering if I did.

The whole weekend, I went over the conference again and again in my head trying to think if I had said anything; anything at all that might have leaked and I kept coming up empty handed. I didn't know what would happen, and I was angry, and hurt, and confused at the same time. Had I done something wrong? Should I have told? I didn't know what to do. My answer came that Monday when I returned for another week. I didn't get to see her class until the afternoon and our paths didn't really cross until then. Then she approached with another, as I was standing in the hall. She nonchalantly said, "I know what you did. I'm sorry, I didn't know. Thank you." She might disagree that she said that, but that made my week. I had no doubts that week that I had done the right thing. But that wasn't the end, by a long shot. We met again just last week as she had a break from medical school. Many conversations would follow. There would be many things we would disagree on, but the honesty would remain. Medical school, who would've thought. I said that a teacher affects eternity, but I would be remiss if I didn't say the opposite is true as well.

CHAPTER TWENTY-TWO

Transformation

1

We were rounding the last leg of the tour. This final walk was nearing the end. "Now remember, don't kick it hard because, I ain't going down in that sewer drain again. You always kick it down there in the weeds, and I think that's where I got that poison." It's funny because we had been through many of these sewer drains. It wasn't enough to go above ground anymore, we wanted to explore underground. You travel past these grates and manholes all the time, and even look down on occasion, but we were there. We traveled some of the underground passages. To tell you the truth, there's not too much to them. We didn't run into too many critters, or stinky stuff, but lots of spiders. This was an area where the storm drain opened up, and the ball always seemed to find its way down there. These were some of the last kicks we would make. It was getting late now, and I did have a big day tomorrow.

"Go ahead…make the kick and stop fooling around. That's 'delay of game' you know." I went ahead and kicked. The ball floated, for what seemed like forever and hit the corner of the curb, bounced straight up and hit again. "Score!" It was double. We were tied now, and the game was going into overtime. "Lucky shot." Tony paused just kicking the ball between his feet. "Don't you worry about getting lonely? I mean, you're not going to be married, and you'll have your own church, so you'll be alone." "I thought about that. I know there's a difference between being 'lonely' and being 'alone.' My personality is such that I need some time alone, no doubt about it. But I imagine I could get lonely at times. Do you ever get lonely?" Tony laughed. "I'm never alone!" "Yeah, but I mean, not necessarily alone, but lonely…like, isolated or detached." "What do you mean?" "I mean, like you're not connected, or that no one understands you, or that you're in this alone." "Well, not like that really. I get times when I'm down, or depressed, but it's not like being lonely. I don't know. I just think you might be lonely at times." "I imagine I could be too. But it's different now. There was a time when I really couldn't handle that too well." "When were you like that? I don't remember that." "Well, I didn't tell you. As far as you knew, all was right in the world." "What? Why didn't you tell me? You know you could trust me. You keepin' stuff from me now?" "It wasn't a question of trust… it was a question of figuring things out for myself. Another friend helped me with that, in a way you couldn't have. And the irony is, she didn't even know it."

2

I decided while I was in high school, that the possibility existed that I might be a priest (I know, what were the chances right?). Therefore, I was not going to involve myself with the drug scene or alcohol and all the things that go with the parties in high school and college. I stuck to this and was very devoted to the possibility that this might happen. The problem with such a pledge is that one might fall into something far worse than any of those things I was avoiding. And that is exactly what happened to me.

You see, when you take all of these things out of your life, and don't associate with people who do such things, you set yourself up as the judge and arbiter. You become the judge of everyone who does these things, and that is what I did. It wasn't enough that I isolated myself from these people, but I condemned them, and reduced them to the worst thing they did. And because of this, I became an island unto myself, and I was miserable. I remember such depression as I never felt before, and pray I never feel again. I was absolutely alone. I remember some evenings praying for death. Yeah, I prayed for death. Oh, I still prayed… but for death. And then one night, I will never forget.

Once again, I was praying for death. It was about midnight and the phone rang. It was a friend of mine across campus, and she was ill and wanted me to walk her to the health center. The health center was across campus in the other direction, but begrudgingly I did (I mean, she *was* one of my only friends at that point). We arrived at the center, and I waited in the room outside of the offices. Finding myself with nothing to do but wait, I picked up a Reader's Digest and opened to "Quotable Quotes." There was a quote from a Louis L'Amore novel at the bottom of the page. I read the quote, and for a moment it was like time stopped. And everything changed in that moment. I looked around to make sure I was alone and tore the page from the book. And up to a year ago, I still had the page framed in my office. I recently lent it out to someone who needed it more than I. From that moment, my life changed forever. I made the decision that never again would I judge anyone, but would try to see the best in them. And in seeing the best in others, perhaps for the first time in a long time, I saw the best in myself as well. The confidence that I never had became a part of me, and the insecurities, and doubts evaporated like a summer dew. It was amazing. The scars of those experiences remain, and yet as I said before, some scars remind us of the moment we changed…the moment I began a new future.

3

"Tomorrow, I begin a new future." "You mean today. It's after twelve. What's your curfew?" We laughed. "Go ahead. All you have to do is make this corner shot and you're home free." That was the phrase right? We had joked about this for years and now finally something had come of it. I eyed up the corner, doing commentary the whole way. "This is it folks. All she wrote. If he makes the corner hit from the grass, it's 'good-night Irene' for Tony." "You're right Gorilla Monsoon, this is gonna be sink or swim for Mike. He's not too good under pressure." "What do you mean I'm not good under pressure? 'Sit down on that chair right there and le-me show you how it's done.'" I was ready for the kick. "Home free," he said.

4

I suppose he was going to use his "Indian Navajo Powers" as well. But when you think about it, the phrase encapsulates our lives. We *were* free. Think about it. When you're a baby, you're free, but really not. I mean, you're free of the worries of the world, because if someone's not changing one end they're feeding another. If they're not talking "baby talk" to you or telling you how cute you are, they're bouncing you on their knee or patting you on the back to get a burp. Ironic, isn't it, that they work so hard to get you to burp when you're young, and work even harder to get you not to, when you're old. They're always stripping you down as a baby, and trying to cover every square inch of you when you're a teen. They try to get you to walk and talk and then can't keep you in the house, or off the phone, or quiet in church. We are strange creatures. And yet…Tony and I *were* free.

We did much of what we wanted to do, and those things we were prevented from doing, weren't really that important to us. We were limited only by the boundaries of imagination, and yet there were no boundaries. We shared everything; lived it all together in the best times of our lives, and we did it where we knew the people, the traditions, the places; this little part of creation for us was home. It will always be home. "Home Free" wasn't just a catch phrase that was a trigger for trouble, or even a traditional battle cry, so much as it was the phrase that captured our spirits and described our character like nothing else could.

5

I made the kick and as I did, a guy yelled out the window. "Hey, shut up out there. People are trying to sleep. Damn kids." I couldn't muzzle him fast enough. "It's a free country. We're not hurting anything." Did he just say that? What was he, fifteen again? We were both thirty! Were we scared of this guy? Did he know who we were? "Margaret, call the police. Stay right there, I'm coming out." This was a perfect damper to a perfectly good evening. "We're going now (and Tony called the man something that was appropriate, but not acceptable, for which he would later add on, 'sorry Dear Lord')". We began to walk away, and the man came outside dressed in his plaid bathrobe and slippers, like he just walked off the set of the "Brady Bunch." I just paused, waiting for Alice and the gang to follow, but he stood there and with a bit of hesitancy in his voice said: "You *better* go." Tony stopped in his tracks. All that crossed my mind were the thoughts, "Come on man, we were both adults here, I was going to be a deacon the next day, don't get into anything tonight." He looked at the guy and let out his traditional Tony "machine-gun" laugh, and the guy was speechless. We walked away.

I don't remember whether I made the last point or not. Neither does Tony, although, he claims to this day he won the game. Whether he won the game or not really didn't matter too much at all that night. What mattered was that two men, who met on a September day, twenty-four years ago, still loved each other enough to say "brother." Two grown men could still walk the streets of their home, kicking a ball and reminiscing about the freedom of youth, and the treasure of friendship.

And there were no tears. What is it Dr. Suess said: "Don't cry because it's over; smile because it happened." We knew it wasn't over. It was just the prologue to another book: perhaps, Another Twenty-four Years. And Hattman wouldn't be there; hopefully neither would weapon-wielding Amish, or broken wrists. But with imagination, one can never tell. This was not the end by any stretch of the imagination. I smiled as we walked to our cars and said "goodnight"...or "good morning", but not "goodbye". And the quote from Louie L'Amore that saved my life years before in the health center, at the turning point in my life came to mind, as true that night as it ever was: "There will come a time when you believe everything is finished...that will be the beginning."[1]

Afterward

We're not done yet…this is important.

Suffering is one of the unsolved mysteries of the universe. There appears to be no rhyme or reason, and theodicy, the philosophical concept of why bad things happen to good people continues to plague us. The writing of this book has been a life-long work for Tony and me. We've told these stories hundreds of times, to countless individuals before finally writing them down. We've laughed and cried and laughed some more in our palavers over what "really happened" and who would look bad in the situation. Now begins another book in our anthology called life.

I am now a priest and have experienced the suffering of people in a way I never thought possible. I recall at one point during my priesthood, encountering a person who was so wrought with psychological pain that I just couldn't possibly understand. I remember praying that evening that God would allow me true compassion or "suffering with" the person; that I might get a glimpse into their world. The next morning He granted my request…one that I will never make again. I don't remember much about the day, but I sat in a chair for most of it, unable to move; wallowing in such pain and solitude that I was almost willing to do anything to escape it. Thank God, the day eventually ended and all was back to normal the next day. I have been given the gift of detachment; the ability to separate my own life and pain from those I experience through the eyes of others on a daily basis. It seems to get more difficult by the day, and yet as long as I keep myself grounded, I can seemingly leave those things on the hook, as I hang up my cassock. But not this time.

Tony is suffering from an illness, and therefore, so am I. The worst thing about an illness is not knowing exactly what it is. If I know I have cancer, I know what the symptoms are, and what the treatment is like, and have some anticipation of what I will meet. But Tony is different. From all the symptoms, it appears he has a rare disease of the joints, muscles, and bones. They are not calling it multiple myoloma although they are using some medications as though it were. At this point, they have called it MGUS. Monoclonal gammopathy of uncertain significance (MGUS) is a common, age-related medical condition characterized by an accumulation of bone marrow plasma cells derived from a single abnormal clone. Although Tony has been treated time and again by experts in various places, he continues to move like a man twice his age. I fear, as I know he does, that this creature will steal his life.

I have learned to detach from pain and suffering in a way that it won't affect the job I know I must do; and yet I cannot remove the weight on my heart. Viktor Frankl would say that suffering breaks the illusion we live in and pares us down to what is most authentically human about us: our ability to love…even those we do not know (Frankl, Viktor E. Man's Search for Meaning. 3rd ed. New York: Simon and Schuster, 1984). I would agree with his assertion, in that, although Tony has never had trouble loving, he would sometimes get caught up in the worries of the things he didn't have…we all do. And yet now I see about him a certain peace I had not witnessed before. He wants to make sure his family is taken care of, but he is not out to be a millionaire; he is not out to be a success by the standards of this world; he wants only the best for those he loves. And so by Frankl's definition, I would say suffering has successfully done that for him…but not for me.

It's interesting that most of the people I speak to are saddened by the loss of a loved one…but petrified about their own death. In my case, it's eerily the opposite: I am ready to go any time, but am not nearly ready to lose my best friend. I'll admit I didn't think about it so much at first, because as a scientist myself, I know the technology out there, especially in pharmaceuticals. But the medicines didn't help. I was still concerned, but it didn't seem so imminent, and he was still seeing doctors, so I waited patiently. I think it finally hit me when we had time to talk. In a world where he was traveling for sales and I was going all the time, that was a rare opportunity, and as I said in the book, when he spoke, I listened. It was a somber conversation about death. And I found myself unable to be the priest counselor or consoler; I found myself inconsolable, even in the midst of his attempts to soften it or make it sound less painful.

I bring this up in the afterward, not to drag you down, but simply to make a point. Tony made it quite clear that he admired me for all I'd done; for all my studies and gifts and successes. The irony is that all of those experiences never prepared me for the impending loss of my blood brother. The irony is that the one who took none of those classes; the one who doesn't know the languages or the histories or necessarily have the background; that one, has ministered to me, and consoled me in a way that I thought seemingly impossible. Therefore, the irony of this book, is that it was written through my thoughts and words (like many of his reports back in grade school) but the voice that echoes "Home Free" through these pages, and the meaning of that mantra, are clearly his own.

(Endnotes)
1 L'Amore, Louis: Lonely on the Mountain. Bantam books, 1984.